'SINCE O'CASEY' AND OTHER ESSAYS
ON IRISH DRAMA

IRISH LITERARY STUDIES

'SINCE O'CASEY'
AND OTHER ESSAYS
ON IRISH DRAMA

Robert Hogan

Irish Literary Studies 15

1983
COLIN SMYTHE
Gerrards Cross, Bucks.

BARNES AND NOBLE BOOKS
Totowa, New Jersey

Copyright © 1983 by Robert Hogan

First published in 1983 by Colin Smythe Limited
Gerrards Cross, Buckinghamshire

British Library Cataloguing in Publication Data

Hogan, Robert
'Since O'Casey' and other essays on Irish drama.
—(Irish literary studies ISSN 0140-895X; 15)
1. English drama—Irish authors
2. English drama—20th century
I. Title   II. Series
822'.91209   PR37

ISBN 0-86140-115-8

First published in the United States of America in 1983
by Barnes and Noble Books, 81 Adams Drive, Totowa,
N.J. 07512

Library of Congress Cataloging in Publication Data

Hogan, Robert Goode, 1930—
'Since O'Casey' and other essays on Irish drama.
(Irish literary studies; 15)
Includes bibliographical references and index.
1. English drama—20th century—History and criticism.
2. English drama—20th century—History and criticism.
3. Ireland in literature.
4. O'Casey, Sean, 1880-1964—Criticism and interpretation.
I. Title.   II. Series.
PR8789.H64   1983   822'.91'099415   82-22813

ISBN 0-389-20346-7 (Barnes and Noble)

PR
8789
H64
1983

Printed in Great Britain
Set by Grove Graphics, Tring, Herts.,
and printed from copy supplied and bound by
Billing & Sons Ltd., Worcester

To Michael Molloy,
John O'Donovan and James Douglas

CONTENTS

PREFACE

About fifteen years ago, I published a book called *After the Irish Renaissance,* which was described as 'a critical History of the Irish Drama since *The Plough and the Stars.'* This book is something of a sequel to and a broadening of that earlier one. It is a sequel to, inasmuch as the title chapter continues the story by being a factual and, I hope, justly critical account of what important has happened since the earlier book. But more interesting — to me at least — is that this present book is a broadening of the critical base, or an addition to the critical stances, of the earlier one. Although the title chapter continues the method of critical history (or, to be pejorative, the academic journalism) of the earlier volume, the other chapters take other views.

The other views comprise such traditional approaches as biography and history and the weighing of influence, but they also include some approaches more usually utilised in the criticism of poetry or fiction. These approaches are sometimes broadly generic, sometimes specifically structural, and frequently minutely rhetorical. In modern times, a close contemplation of language has become a commonplace of the criticism of lyrical poetry. Such close scrutiny has rarely been applied to plays, for the obvious reason that plays are just enormously longer than sonnets. This approach, of what was a generation or so ago called the New Criticism, has, of course, been directed towards plays; but it has really been directed in their rehearsal rather than in their criticism. In rehearsal, under the scrutiny of a canny director, everything in a play — every nuance and every intonation — is minutely examined and explored. In printed criticism of drama, there is simply not the space; and a book like *Stanislavsky Rehearses Othello* or Robert B. Heilman's *This Great Stage* on *Lear* is rare in its meticulous scrutiny. This present book, which discusses a multitude of plays, can naturally adopt such a meticulous investigation only sporadically. Nevertheless, the book frequently attempts to be sporadic. Whether the mixture of these various approaches adds up to coherence is, of course, a matter to be judged by the judicious reader.

Some of the material here appeared first somewhere else; and I have sometimes slightly, but usually hugely, revised it. A version of the chapter on Synge appeared first in *Sunshine and the Moon's Delight, a Centenary Tribute to John Millington Synge,* edited by S. B. Bushrui, and published by Colin Smythe and the American University of Beirut in 1972. However, some portions of the Synge chapter, which deal with George Fitzmaurice, are culled from a lecture given at the Listowel Writers' Week in 1977. 'O'Casey, the Style and the Artist' first appeared in an O'Casey issue of *The James Joyce Quarterly,* edited by Bernard Benstock about 1970. 'O'Casey, the Style and the Man' was a talk in the Thomas Davis lectures on Radio Éireann; it was commissioned by Micheál Ó hAodha and appeared in his *The O'Casey Enigma* published by the Mercier Press in 1980. 'The Influence of O'Casey' was an essay commissioned by Christopher Murray for an O'Casey number of *The Irish University Review* which appeared in the Spring of 1980. 'Denis Johnston's Horse Laugh' was commissioned by Joseph Ronsley for a collection of essays on Johnston which was published by Colin Smythe in 1981. Some paragraphs of 'Trying to Like Beckett' appeared in my Beckett article in *The Dictionary of Irish Literature*, published by Greenwood Press in 1979. Portions of 'Since O'Casey' appeared in my essay 'Where Have all the Shamrocks Gone?' included in *Aspects of the Irish Theatre,* edited by Patrick Rafroidi and others, and published by the University of Lille sometime in the early 1970s. Other portions were part of a talk called 'The Virile Dead,' given to the American Theatre Association in New York, also sometime in the early 1970s. To all of these individuals and organizations, my thanks for prodding me to think, and my hopes that the present considerable rethinking constitutes an improvement.

Robert Hogan
Newark, Delaware
August, 1982

YEATS CREATES A CRITIC

Dublin is a little city and a cliquish one. In the early years of this century, one clique of literary people became interested in the theatre and inaugurated the movement now know as the Irish Dramatic Renaissance. The notable members of this clique were initially W. B. Yeats, Lady Gregory, George Moore, Edward Martyn and Douglas Hyde. But Dublin is also a volatile city, and yesterday's allies are often today's enemies. Predictably, then, the Irish Literary Theatre clique dissolved in three short years. Moore and Martyn and Hyde went, or were pushed, on their own ways, and W. B. Yeats found new allies in a group of amateur actors headed by the brothers Fay, in a group of patriotic women headed by Maud Gonne, and in a group of young writers headed, more or less, by his old friend George Russell. And in a very short time, this clique broke up into − .

There is no need to tell again a well-known story, but much of the fascination of Irish literary history lies in the charting of an ever-shifting pattern of momentary alliances − around Yeats or AE or Arthur Griffith or, later, Robert Smyllie and the Pearl Bar, or Patrick Kavanagh and McDaid's, or Brendan Behan and the Catacombs. However, there is one small clique that has always been overlooked. Its core was not actors or painters or writers, although it did include the occasional writer like T. C. Murray or actor like F. J. McCormick. Its true core was a group of self-made, self-taught, and totally unacademic scholars, critics and historians of the theatre.

Chief among these men were D. J. O'Donoghue who wrote a biographical dictionary of the poets of Ireland and a life of Carleton, and who was the prolific editor of Carleton, Lover, Mangan, Thomas Davis and others; Joseph Holloway, the diarist and collector of theatrical memorabilia; Frank Fay, the actor and verse speaker and voice coach; and W. J. Lawrence. Of these four, the closest in interest and in friendship were Holloway, Fay and Lawrence. All three were avid readers, talkers and walkers. Holloway, for instance, remembered on the occasion of Lawrence's death that:

He was a tremendous worker all his life and the spade-work knowledge

11

he had accumulated placed him on the pinnacle of Elizabethan researches. He was one of those rare human beings with a love for research in theatrical history, who was an enthusiastic playgoer as well. . . . He was the straightest man I ever knew, and as honest in his expression of opinion as one could possibly be. He left Dublin some eight years ago never to return; for thirty years and more he and I met at least once a week, and had a walk and a talk usually down by the Pigeon House Road; and, oh, what a wealth of information he poured into my eagerly listening ear as we walked along, with the ever-changing sea on one side of us and the Dublin mountains with the sun's chasing the shadows softly up their sides on the other.[1]

Or, as Frank Fay's son, Gerard, wrote in 1936:

I can remember long walks on Dun Laoghaire Pier with Mr. Lawrence and my father, during which they discoursed at great length, and in considerable detail on matters of theatre history. In the intervals between trying to catch hornies on a bent pin, and throwing stones at the gulls, I used to join them and listen to the talk. The feature of Mr. Lawrence's conversation that I can most clearly remember is his ability to talk of serious things, dry matters, in an entertaining way. Mr. Lawrence is now Dr. Lawrence, and the subjects which seemed dry to me, then, are now vital and important, but the same quality is in the book that I found in the conversations long ago.[2]

These three friends — the playgoer Holloway, the actor Fay and the scholar Lawrence — shared a common avidity about the theatre and an encyclopaedic knowledge of its history and traditions. Holloway was the most prolific writer of the three, and his basic diary reaches some twenty-five million words. He was, however, a private writer who published mainly chatty bits of journalism, but who rightly regarded his diary, his teeming notebooks of factual data and his massive collection of theatre memorabilia as a source or quarry for some future historian. One goes to Holloway not for his personality which was benevolently bland, and not for his style which is usually dreadful, but for facts — facts in abundance, a teeming plethora of minutiae that may be mined by the industrious grubber from his avalanche of words.

Frank Fay was the least prolific writer of the three friends. He began his career as an amateur actor whose infatuation with the stage led him into voracious reading and then into critical journalism for Arthur Griffith's *Sinn Fein*. Fay's published criticism curiously resembles Bernard Shaw's. The resemblance is not in its quality of content and certainly not in its facility of expression, but in its tactics. Like Shaw, Fay had a vision of the kind of theatre he wanted, and his critical pieces are basically an attack upon the Irish drama and Irish acting of his day. Primarily, he tilted at the conventional melodramatic acting of the conventional neo-Boucicault Irish repertoire of the early 1900s. His own standards, evolved from reading about Andre Antoine and Ole Bull, and from seeing what French companies came to Dublin, pushed him to develop a theory of acting for Irish actors in an Irish national theatre. Many of his ideas dovetailed with the slowly shaping predilections about drama of W. B. Yeats, and when Fay's letters to Yeats are finally publish- ed they will show how influential his thinking was on the poet's theory and dramatic practice. The creation of the Abbey Theatre, of course, gave Fay a full-time occupation and a platform on which to test his theories; and his critical writing then virtually ceased. After his rupture with the Abbey in 1908 and after several subsequent seasons of touring with provincial Shakespearean companies, his interests were almost entirely diverted to the speaking of Shakespearean verse and to the coaching of vocal technique in Dublin.

The most meticulous researcher and the only consistently publishing writer among the three friends was W. J. Lawrence. From a prodigious amount of early journalism, he graduated to critical reviewing and then to scholarly articles and books. After the publica- tion in 1912 and 1913 of his two volumes entitled *The Elizabethan Playhouse,* he came to be recognised as an original researcher of extraordinary merit. With many subsequent volumes, he solidified his reputation as a leading historian of the Elizabethan stage; and in his last years he was the recipient of many awards and accolades. In 1927, for instance, T. S. Eliot wrote of him:

The name of Mr. W. J. Lawrence stands very high in contemporary scholarship of Elizabethan drama. In the scholarship of textual criticism he has several equals, and a few superiors; but in the particular field of these two books [*Pre-Restoration Stage Studies* and *The Physical Condition of the Elizabethan Public Playhouse*] he is easily ahead in learning, in fertility of conjecture, and in the variety and interest of his topics. He seems to have read, with great pains, a greater number of inferior sixteenth and seven- teenth century plays than anyone living: and out of this mass of matter, and from other sources, he has arrived nearer than anyone towards the reconstruction of the conditions under which Elizabethan plays were played.

Such praise was echoed by many others, including Allardyce Nicoll, Bonamy Dobree, J. Dover Wilson, Leslie Hotson, Lily B. Camp- bell and John Livingstone Lowes. This acceptance by eminent academics of a man who had made his way entirely alone and entirely outside of academe is remarkable testimony to Lawrence's rare tenacity and high achievement.

There was nothing in Lawrence's background to suggest the bent that his career would take. He was born in Belfast on October 29, 1862, the son of a manager of a railway hotel and cafe, and he could look forward to nothing other than a commercial career and to leaving his formal academic training in his middle teens. His primary education was at the Dowager Countess of Annesley's private school at Newcastle, and then he became a boarder at the Belfast Methodist College from 1872 to 1878. The only glimpse of the young Lawrence in these years is a remark, years later, by an old schoolmate: 'Of the boarders of that time I remember, among others, W. J. Lawrence. . . . I remember Lawrence going from room to room, in and out of school hours, with an ink-bottle and pen in his hand, a forecast of his literary career.' However, in an interview published in *The Weekly Irish Times* in 1912, on the occasion of the publication *The Elizabethan Playhouse,* is the further information that Lawrence's own 'most vivid recollection of that period is of the six weeks solitary confinement he received for breaking bounds with a boy chum and roaming down town to the theatre to see a performance of *Nicholas Nickleby.*'

On leaving school, Lawrence served a commercial apprenticeship with Messrs, Kirker Green and Company of Belfast. Already his consuming interest was the stage, and in 1878, at the age of sixteen, he published his first contributions to stage history in the ephemeral *Belfast Magazine.* Dan Lowrey, who was the proprietor at that time of the Alhambra Music Hall, included this — as Lawrence described it — 'little magazine of literary pretensions as a supplement to the weekly programme'.

In 1899, Lawrence married Florence Fanny Bradley, and became a clerk and commercial traveller in the wine and spirit trade for the Comber Distillery, a task he remained at for thirteen years. A companion of these years later wrote:

> I knew him well when he lived in Ulster. He was one of a little circle which met in a house in Alfred Street and discussed literary matters. Even then he was known as an authority on all things pertaining to the stage at the times of Elizabeth and the Restoration. Sir Frank Benson, who sometimes visited us, looked up to Mr. Lawrence with great respect for his stage lore. At that time — more than thirty years ago — Mr. Lawrence did not live in Comber, but in Newcastle, County Down. He was an intimate friend of Mr. Robert Cromie, the scientific novelist and essayist, and of Mr. Louis M'Quilland, who now occupies a prominent place in literary circles in London.

There are in the Lawrence papers perhaps half a dozen published short stories which he wrote in collaboration with Cromie. Usually

Lawrence supplied the plotting and Cromie the writing. None is of particular interest.

Already Lawrence was publishing feature articles on the drama in newspapers, and in 1892 he published by subscription his first book, *The Life of Gustavus Vaughan Brooke, Tragedian.* This was followed in 1893 by a short volume, *Barry Sullivan: A Biographical Sketch,* about the recently deceased nineteenth century tragedian so much admired by Bernard Shaw. This was followed by a much more ambitious and still unpublished work, *The Annals of the Old Belfast Stage.* For this book, his research took him meticulously through the crumbling files of innumerable old newspapers and journals, and the labour solidified his method of painstaking grubbing among original sources for the stray fact. His earlier G. V. Brooke volume had been subsidized out of his own pocket, and he finally lost about £20 on it. *The Old Belfast Stage* was similarly advertised in a brochure of late 1896, which stated that the projected volume would be available to subscribers in early February, 1897, in an edition of 250 copies and at a price of 10/6. Unfortunately only thirty-six subscribers appeared, and so the project was abandoned. The manuscript, with various illustrative material and much later corrective marginalia, ultimately found its way to the National Library of Ireland.

Lawrence was now sufficiently known to be engaged to write short biographies of older-day actors for *The Dictionary of National Biography.* Thus encouraged, he gave up his job, and, in his own words:

After spending my time from November 1902 in purposeful research in the British Museum (lodging meanwhile for the most part in Doughty Street, W.C.) I found myself in the following spring at the end of my pecuniary resources, and was thankful to take an offer of £3 a week to go to Dublin as advertisement writer for an Electropathic Institute opened in Kildare Street by an Irish-American quack who called himself Macara (real name McCarthy). For six whole weeks I devised taking advertisements for the Saturday evening papers (notably the *Evening Telegraph*), and then, as gulls came in none too satisfactorily, I was cashiered. While with Macara I lived on the premises, my wife meanwhile being in Belfast with a relative; but, on leaving his services I took apartments in Lower Fitzwilliam Street, and my wife then joined me. I then began a fruitful journalistic career in Dublin, and devoted my leisure time to research into the history of the old Dublin stage.

Synge and I came to Dublin much about the same time, and I saw his first two plays, 'In the Shadow of the Glen' and 'Riders to the Sea' produced late in 1903 at the Molesworth Hall.

Arrived in Dublin about May 1903.

R. Crompton Rhodes, the editor of Richard Brinsley Sheridan, speaks of Lawrence's passion for research. It truly was a passion, for during Lawrence's longest stay in Dublin, from 1903 to 1916, he was also engaged in journalism for a Dublin paper, he was the Dublin correspondent and reviewer for *The Stage,* and he was a prolific freelance contributor to Irish, English, Continental and American periodicals, writing for a range of audience that embraced the man in the street and the scholar in the study. As a reviewer, his outspoken, even vituperative opinions led him into several confrontations with the Abbey Theatre and with W. B. Yeats, but also during this time he was quietly laying the foundations for his scholarly reputation. Those labours culminated in the publication in 1912 and 1913, by A.H. Bullen of the Shakespeare Head Press, of his two volumes entitled *The Elizabethan Playhouse and Other Studies.* During the same period, Lawrence was devoting several hours a day for five days a week to compiling the complete annals of the Dublin stage. These last copious papers were eventually sold to the University of Cincinnati Library.

In 1916, shaken by the Rising, Lawrence moved to America where he remained for two years and three months. He lived in New Jersey, and his stay was not entirely happy or profitable, although in late 1917 he did go on a lecture tour, speaking at Yale, Harvard, Columbia and several universities in the Middle West. His profit for the tour was only $376, and, as *The Belfast News-Letter* later put it,'. . . other totally unliterary occupations were vital . . . to keep alive. Hence, he worked successively as typist in a rubber reclaiming factory, storekeeper in munition works, and even as packer in a chemical manufactory.'

When Lawrence returned with much relief to Dublin in 1919, he resumed his reviewing for *The Stage,* but by this time his scholarship was bringing him increasing renown, and he was able to curtail his journalism. In 1922 he was aided by a Civil List Pension 'for services to the history and literature of the drama'; and, with this money, he was able to take a sabbatical from reviewing and journalism and to spend nine months during 1923 in Oxford reading at the Bodleian. When he returned to Dublin at the end of the year, he brought his library with him, remarking that it comprised 'half a ton of books.'

In 1925 and 1926 he spent a few months again in America, but on this pleasanter occasion he was a visiting lecturer at Harvard, and his lectures were published in 1927 by Harvard University Press under the title of *The Physical Conditions of the Elizabethan Public Playhouse.* In the same year the press accompanied this slim scholarly

volume with the more substantial *Pre-Restoration Stage Studies.*
In 1928 Basil Blackwell brought out his *Shakespeare's Workshop,*
and in that same year his wife's increasing ill health forced him reluc-
tantly to move from Dublin to the South of England.

In 1920 he had been elected a Fellow of the Royal Society of
Literature in recognition of his work as a Shakespeare scholar, and
in 1931 Queen's University, Belfast, awarded him a D. Litt. In the
meantime, there were more books: *Those Nut-Cracking Elizabethans*
and *Old Theatre Days and Ways* in 1925, *Speeding Up Shakespeare*
in 1937.

It is pleasant to think that the encomiums and honours had the
effect of mellowing Lawrence from the intractable, red-bearded man
who was constantly leaping up in meetings in the early years of the
century to contradict W. B. Yeats. And actually there is some
evidence for thinking that he had mellowed. In 1936, L. C. Knights
gave a somewhat carping and rather muddled review of *Those Nut-
Cracking Elizabethans* in *The London Mercury,* and Lawrence simply remarked in his notebook that 'There was a notice also of my
book . . . by a Mr. Knights, who gave me the impression of being
a trifle dazed.'

Lawrence's wife had been for many years an invalid, and she died
in November 1938, at the age of seventy-five. Lawrence too was in
failing health. In 1938, *The Belfast News-Letter* noted that he was
having an operation for a cataract and that he had been unable to
work for several years. Most of his library, that had not already been
sent to Cincinnati, was listed in a book-seller's catalogue in August,
1939.

In 1940, however, in view of his 'valuable services to Theatrical
and Dramatic History,' he was elected an Honorary Member of the
London Critics Circle, and on the same day he received a D. Litt.
from the National University of Ireland. *The Belfast News-Letter*
remarked that 'Failing eyesight, which will prevent him from travel
ling to Dublin on March 7, has not dimmed the ardour of his spirit,
and, but for the outbreak of war, he would now be publishing his
already completed *Shakespeare's Lost Hamlet,* a little volume which
he values beyond all he has yet printed, and which, it is said,
embodies a prime Shakespearean discovery.'

J. J. Hogan's address, on the occasion of the honorary degree
from the National University, is in many ways an apt summation
of Lawrence's character and scholarly career:

His knowledge of detail, his deftness in bringing it to bear on a disputed
point, is unrivalled. Mr Lawrence is not, like many masters of detail, a

pedant. The very titles of his books give a promise of freshness and unconventionality which is justified by the contents, so that raking among the dry dust of the Elizabethan greenroom becomes as entertaining to us as it is to him. But the pleasure would soon flag if Mr. Lawrence were simply an exhibitor of entertaining details. He uses them as befits a serious scholar. At any moment, we shall find him making bold inferences from them, and attempting to settle some important open question which perhaps, because it was difficult, the critics had conspired to ignore. No doubt, Mr. Lawrence may sometimes be misled by his courage; but such errors, because they lead towards knowledge, are better than a safe timidity.

To that, one need perhaps only add these remarks from the London *Times:*

> His special contribution to learning was his insistence that no drama, and least of all Elizabethan drama, could be understood without a minute knowledge of the theatre and the stage, and of all theatrical custom and usage. Unconventional, unhampered by academic or personal loyalties, and as shrewd as he was laborious, he blew away, in book after book, large quantities of conjecture and error, and left very little of his own for future students to blow away. He was a first-rate lecturer. . . and his enthusiasm and his generosity in sharing his knowledge won him many friends.[3]

Attached to the rear endpaper of Lawrence's final Personal Clippings Book is a typed note whose one or two misspellings attest to his growing blindness:

> Finished at the Malvern House, 176 the Rye, Dulwich, S.E. 22, in the Spring of 1940.
> With this bool ends a not ineventful literary and journalistic career of over a half a century's duration.
> EXIT W.J. LAWRENCE

In August, 1940, he died.

II

In the Preface to his 1935 volume, *Old Theatre Days and Ways,* Lawrence rather ruefully noted that:

> Unfortunately, profuse as have been my contributions to periodical literature on a great variety of theatrical subjects, that fact has been little recognized. Aristides was no more wearied over being characterized as the Just than I am over being classified solely as an Elizabethan scholar. It is

true that for many years Shakespeare's stage has had for me its persistent fascinations, but not to the exclusion of other interests. The whole theatre has been my province.[4]

La Tourette Stockwell and William Smith Clark have testified to Lawrence's generosity and encouragement in their work on the early Irish stage, about which Lawrence himself had done a huge amount of preliminary research. Indeed, Professor Clark's bibliography in his *The Irish Stage in the Country Towns* lists more than fifty published articles by Lawrence in various Irish journals. Lawrence's activity, however, was not concerned solely with the theatre of the 17th, the 18th or the 19th centuries. He was intermittently, for twenty-five or thirty years, a reviewer of the current Irish theatre, and it is these forgotten critical pieces that I am mainly interested in here.

Lawrence first came to Dublin in 1903, and so he witnessed the Irish dramatic movement almost from its inception, through all of its great years, up until really the emergence of Sean O'Casey. In other words, he had both great plays and great players to write about. These were the fruitful years of Yeats, Synge, Lady Gregory, George Fitzmaurice, St. John Ervine, Lord Dunsany, Lennox Robinson, T. C. Murray, George Shiels and, of course, O'Casey. These years saw the first productions of *The Playboy of the Western World* and *Riders to the Sea,* of *The Gaol Gate* and *The Workhouse Ward,* of *The Pie-Dish,* of *The Glittering Gate,* of *Thomas Muskerry* and *Maurice Harte* and *John Ferguson,* of *The Magic Glasses* and *The Whiteheaded Boy* and *Paul Twyning,* and of *The Shadow of a Gunman* and *Juno and the Paycock.* And these years also saw the greatest of Irish players — Frank and Willie Fay, Sara Allgood and Maire O'Neill, Arthur Sinclair and J. M. Kerrigan and Fred O'Donovan, and, then later, the consummate F. J. McCormick and the inimitable Barry Fitzgerald. If there was ever a time for the emergence of a great drama critic, these were the years. Lawrence, unfortunately, was not a great drama critic, but he was the closest approach that Dublin offered.

There are probably several reasons why this man who trained himself to be a great scholar could not train himself to be a great drama critic, but I am inclined to think that the chief reason was W. B. Yeats. In one of the pages of his Personal Cuttings book, Lawrence wrote:

One might say of Yeats what Laborde said of Phillidor the composer in palliation of his stupidity: —
'Gentlemen, my friend here is a truly great man: if he has not a particle of common sense, it is because he is all genius.'

There are two views of Yeats implied here, the admiring and the condemnatory. This ambiguity was not restricted to Lawrence,

Holloway, and O'Donoghue, but was certainly the prevalent view about Yeats in Ireland for all of his public career. For instance, in Miss MacNie's book of cartoons and doggerel, *The Celebrity Zoo,* (3rd edition 1925) the first picture is of a camel with the head of Yeats, a head haughtily tilted toward heaven, and the accompanying verse reads:

> As you survey this Camel, with surprise,
> You'll recognise it as a Nobel Prize,
> When it walks calmly, with uplifted nose,
> I'm *sure* it's nearer Heaven than to its toes.[5]

This view is absolutely typical. From his youthful excursions into politics, through his middle years as literary lion, to his late career as Irish Senator and Grand Old Man, Yeats was generally admitted to be the pre-eminent literary and cultural leader in the country, but the admission was usually made with a grudging bitterness that periodically erupted into vehement denunciations.

Undoubtedly, Yeats himself was much to blame. People like Lawrence and Holloway may really be taken as the visible and vocal embodiment of the cultured, middleclass Irishman. They were not, as has been sometimes suggested, merely parochially narrow and priggishly bourgeois. They were avidly receptive to plans for an Irish national theatre, and they enthusiastically championed some of Yeats' own most esoteric experiments, such as *The Shadowy Waters.* They were, however, at times to grow so ferociously alienated that their criticisms became hysterically bigoted, and significantly increased the difficulties of the theatre.

I suspect that the terrific violence of their reaction is, in no small part, due to Yeats' own public manner. As a public man, Yeats was aloof, haughty and pontifically magisterial, while at the same time he managed often to be deliciously absurd. The stories of his public lectures, which could simultaneously be elevating and asinine, are legion, but they are equalled by innumerable hilarious accounts of his inept vagaries in the theatre. There are other Yeatses, of course – Yeats the intractable man of principle, Yeats the cunning schemer – but the Yeats who appeared as public spokesman for the Irish dramatic movement was, for the Lawrences and Holloways of Ireland, difficult to stomach. A good deal of their irritation was simply personal; spleen, envy, sour grapes and witty denigration exist in any literary milieu, but in Ireland they flourish. To a self-taught man like Lawrence, whose theoretical knowledge of the theatre was enormously larger than Yeats's, this magnificently condescending manner was utterly galling. The smouldering resentment built up partly by Yeats's success in the outside world and partly by his own seeming contempt for his audience was bound occasionally to erupt. A most notable instance, of course, was *The Playboy* riots. It has been little remarked that the play was not so much the reason as the excuse for a vehement protest. And that protest was less against J. M. Synge than it was against W. B. Yeats.

With the exception of Holloway, no man was more vituperative in his condemnation of *The Playboy* than Lawrence. However, both men went out of their way to disassociate Synge from the play. For instance, Holloway notes in his Journal for April 25, 1907, three months after the riots:

> W. J. Lawrence was in and left me two copies of the *New York Dramatic Mirror*. He told me he met Synge in the street and stopped him and had it out with him in a friendly chat. Lawrence told him he had no enmity towards him personally, but a principle was involved in refusing the rights of an audience, which he strongly objected to. Synge said that the Abbey was a subsidised theatre in which the audience had no rights. Lawrence answered back that he thought they were trying to build up a National Theatre and get an audience to support it, but if they only wanted to have a hole and corner sort of show, then no more need be said on the matter. They parted with a friendly shake of the hands . . .[6]

Compare that to the Lawrence who arose at the Abbey Theatre debate on *The Playboy,* and cried, 'I am not going to praise Mr. Yeats to-night. I come to bury Caesar, not to praise him.' Or there is the Lawrence who, in an exchange of letters to the Press with Yeats about the arbitrary selection of the theatre's plays, wound up fulminating that he was absolutely 'spoiling for a fight'. This dislike and distrust was certainly reciprocated by Yeats. When Lawrence and Holloway were among the mourners at Synge's graveside, Yeats saw and resented their presence. Or there is the instance when Yeats, making a speech in London, wryly referred to the irascible, red-haired Ulsterman (Lawrence, of course) who constantly rose up at his Dublin speeches to heckle him. Immediately, a red-haired figure arose from the back of the hall, and called out in a flat Ulster voice, 'I am here!' Or there is the letter, undoubtedly instigated by Yeats, which W. A. Henderson sent to Lawrence, deploring his conduct in the theatre. Lawrence's reply to Henderson has survived:

> Mr. W. J. Lawrence presents his compliments to Mr. W. A. Henderson, and begs to acknowledge the receipt of his minatory epistle of the current date, for which there is absolutely no justification. Mr. D. J. O'Donoghue,

who was on Mr. Lawrence's right hand side, Mr. Joseph Holloway who
was on his left, and Mr. R. J. Hughes who sat immediately behind him,
could assure Mr. Henderson, if interrogated, that Mr. Lawrence's conduct
last night in the Abbey Theatre was never otherwise than seemly.

Mr. Lawrence has no desire to put the directors of the Abbey Theatre
to the humiliating necessity of enlisting the services of spies to watch his
doings in the theatre, and in order that they may possess their souls in quiet
he hereby resigns all right and title to free admission as a Journalist during
the period the present directors and secretary hold office.

However seemly Lawrence's conduct may have been at this occasion, the first production of *Deirdre of the Sorrows,* his irascibility
toward Yeats could not always control his behaviour. For instance,
on November 24, 1911, *The Evening Telegraph* reported a disturbance during a lecture which Nugent Monck had given in the theatre
the previous evening on 'The Rise of the Mystery Play'.

Bright and chatty as it was, it provoked what might have been a regrettable
scene. Mr. Monck was describing 'The Second Shepherd's Play' about to
be produced, and was emphasising the fact that all shepherds in it were
characteristically Yorkshire shepherds. He went on — 'I have no doubt that
there were Yorkshiremen of that day who got up and protested that it was
an insult to draw Yorkshireman like that' —

Immediately a gentleman sitting in the front of the pit said loudly — 'Better
not introduce that.'

Another gentleman at the back of the stalls rose and turned towards the
interrupter saying — 'You must not make a disturbance.'

The first gentleman retorted — 'I will do so if I please.'

Some ladies in the stalls cried 'Put him out,' and there was a movement
from several directions, apparently in obedience to the suggestion, but it
died away before the interrupter was reached.

Meanwhile the lecturer proceeded with hardly a pause, and the incident
ended. . . .

In his personal clippings file for that year, Lawrence notes that, 'Mr.
W. J. Lawrence was the interrupter, and Duncan, of the United Arts
Club, was 'the other gentleman.' And, indeed, Lawrence continued
with a series of hissings and booings and minor disruptions in the
theatre until as late as 1915.

All of this seems regrettably childish and trivial now, but it was
fiercely serious at the time; and I cite it as a sympton of widespread
ill-will against the theatre, ill-will fomented to a large extent, I feel,
by Yeats himself. Lawrence was not, however, a merely unreason-
ing hater. As a scholar and critic, he was impelled to find intellectual justification for a stance into which Yeats had unconsciously
manoeuvered him, and which, without Yeats, he might not have
adopted so extremely.

One half of his view concerned the relation of the audience to the theatre. The view of the theatre was made apparent on many occasions, and most dramatically in the instances of *The Playboy, The Shewing-Up of Blanco Posnet* and *The Plough and the Stars.* The theatre's position was that artistic excellence was a criterion outweighing any others, and that such excellence was going to be judged solely by the directors of the theatre. As Lady Gregory put it, 'He who pays the piper calls the tune'. Lawrence was pushed to the view that the ultimate arbiter of artistic excellence was the audience, and that the theatre's repeated attempts to ram *The Playboy* down the gullet of a resisting audience was intolerable. There was undoubtedly some personal frustration mingled with this view. The above-mentioned exchange of letters with Yeats was nominally an attempt by Lawrence to force the directors to broaden the repertoire. It was also a more than covert attempt to force the directors to broaden the directorate.

Lawrence, in effect, got Yeats momentarily to agree to accept an outside reading panel, composed of knowledgeable and cultivated men who were unconnected with the Abbey. Obviously, Lawrence could hardly put his own name forward, but the unavoidable inference is that he considered himself to be eminently qualified.

The other half of Lawrence's rationale was that of a parochial patriotism and a narrow morality. His Ulster background had given him a puritan sensibility which his wide reading in and devotion to the drama of earlier eras tempered and finally counteracted. However, during his Dublin years his reaction to the 'amorality' of Yeats was a serious critical flaw and affected his judgement of all sorts of plays. He attacked, for instance, St. John Ervine for using the word 'whore' in a play, and even in a reference of his own to the Elizabethan play, *The Honest Whore,* referred to it as *The Honest Wanton.* This tendency made him too tolerant of such pious dramas as those of the Quinteros and also of that interminable and innocuous string of Christmas dramas with which the Abbey afflicted its audience. On the other hand, he could be suspiciously intolerant of what was often innocent. He is, for instance, constantly fulminating against the use of what he called 'the sanguinary epithet.'

In addition to these temperamental and moral disadvantages, Lawrence had other critical flaws. He did not always carry his weight of learning lightly, and sometimes he was almost comically pedantic. For example, he is capable of writing, 'Do we not know that velvet was first mentioned by Joinville in Anno Domini 1272, and that its manufacture cannot have been of much earlier date?' To say the least, it is doubtful that his readers were apprised of the fact.

Another flaw in Lawrence's critical equipment is that he was not, even in his scholarly books, a good writer. His style was almost the antithesis of that of a Shaw, a Beerbohm or a Nathan; and sprinkled throughout his notices are favourite phrases and quotations which become almost clichés. Further, he constantly descends into such cumbrous 'fine' writing as 'devoured by the insatiable maw of oblivion . . . exudation of histrionic genius . . . mystic nebulosity . . . an ambulatory anachronism . . . fluidic individuality . . . the perversity of passion . . . the citadel of fastidiousness and preciosity' — that last phrase being an amazing reference to Dublin.

With such flaws, would Lawrence's criticism be worth dredging up from the yellowing files of old and often well-forgotten journals? The answer, I think, is yes; and the reason basically the one I used when apologetically exhuming Joseph Holloway and Frank Fay. The man, despite his disqualifications, had immense knowledge, and, of course, he was there. There are moments when the curtain of the past is drawn aside in his reviews, and we get a glimpse of what the stage specifically looked like, or what Sally Allgood or Arthur Sinclair actually did. (See the Appendix for a short selection from Lawrence, both good and bad.)

It is curious that, despite how much has been written about the Irish drama, little really is actually known of it. Synge and O'Casey have been written about and written about, and so has Yeats, and so to some extent have Fitzmaurice and a few others. But the Irish drama threw up hundreds of plays, and most often what one would have been seen in the theatre was not a play by Yeats or Synge, but one by F. Sarsfield Sampson, or Mrs. Theodore Maynard, or Walter Riddall, or Victor O'D. Power, or R. J. Ray, or J. Bernard MacCarthy. And unless one knows what their plays were like, one has a most limited view of what the Irish drama was like. *The Playboy* and *Juno* were in a repertory that included *The Rebellion in Ballycullen* and *Regina Eyre* and *The Long Road to Garranbraher, The Prodigal, The Cobweb, The Saint* and *By Word of Mouth*. Most of these plays have never been published and probably should never be. But that is all the more reason for Lawrence's critiques of them to be disinterred. Faulty as they are, his critiques would tell us much that we do not know about the great bulk of Irish drama. If all we know is Synge, we can hardly say with Synge, 'That is all we need to know'.

One thing we do know is that Lawrence would have been a better critic, and perhaps the Irish drama itself would have been somewhat better, had he and Yeats been friends.

THE INFLUENCE OF SYNGE

I

Everyone significant in the Irish theatre knows his Synge. Synge is as inescapable a presence as Bernard Shaw is to the modern English drama or Eugene O'Neill to the American. Yet in recent years Synge is probably more of a vague presence in the background rather than an immediate inspiration. He seems to have congealed into a classic in which one respectfully finds certain universal values applicable at any time and in any country. However, Synge's world has receded, and so the qualities in his plays that had once a shocking immediacy have now dulled with time.

When W. G. Fay first played Christy Mahon, he played him as a wretched, scruffy, insignificant little fellow, and much of the strength of *The Playboy of the Western World* derived from the elevation of this nonentity into heroism. When Conal O'Riordan first revived the play after Synge's death, the role of Christy was taken by Fred O'Donovan, and Christy became tidier, handsomer and more personable. In later years Cyril Cusack and then Donal Donnelly infused their versions of Christy with some of the original spirit, but still this gradual tidying up increased, and the play came to be produced more for the easy laugh than for the chilling grotesquerie. In the early 1960s, for instance, there was a musical version called *The Heart's a Wonder,* which was solely a blend of charm and stage-Irish buffoonery. The Siobhan McKenna film of about the same time blunted the stage-Irish antics, but proceeded even further into blandness with a Christy played by a young actor handsome enough to be a matinée idol. The effective scenes in the film were some romantic ones between Pegeen Mike and Christy, and this was a far cry indeed from Synge's original conception.

This blandness has also been apparent in the recent revivals of Synge at the Abbey Theatre. In the past fifteen years, most of the plays have received new productions in English, and *Riders to the Sea* has even been done in Irish on Aran. All of these productions were done carefully and with taste, and each contained some excellences. Still, none was a particularly thrilling night in the theatre, and probably the best that can be said of all of them was that they

25

were mildly interesting. One could hardly imagine any fledgling playwright in the audience being deeply enough stirred to go and do likewise. Synge has become a part of the revered past. His plays are now historical dramas because the world that they mirror has largely disappeared.

This is an enormous loss, for the qualities that electrified the original audiences of his plays, and the qualities that still can move us in the study, are rare and valuable and eminently needed in the contemporary Irish drama, which is in some danger of becoming simply a reflection of fasionable trends in London or Paris or New York.

I would have no idea how those qualities could be recaptured in any contemporary production of Synge, without doing a gross disservice to the basic qualities of the plays. The plays are so much of a particular time and a particular place, that it would be sacrilegious and probably impossible to transplant them to the present by imposing a contemporary style upon them. *Deirdre* or *The Playboy* done in the Berliner Ensemble manner would be a bit too mindboggling. Nevertheless, Chekhov, who was certainly as deeply rooted in late nineteeth century Russia as Synge was in late nineteenth century Ireland, still holds the boards with undiminished effectiveness. Chekhov does so, though, not in productions which attempt to transplant him to the Deep South of America, but in productions which attempt a minute fidelity to the world Chekhov knew.[1] Perhaps what is needed to revivify the Synge plays for a contemporary audience is a similar close and even naturalistic fidelity, a fidelity which throws into bold relief the sensuality of the plays and their grotesquerie.

II

Determining precise literary influence is at best an imprecise business. In other times when a smaller premium was placed upon originality, it was possible to say with some certainty that Shakespeare borrowed this portion of his plot from Petrarch, or that Boucicault stole this device from Augustin Daly. Nowadays, when most countries are signatories to the Berne convention, copyright laws prevent the more overt kind of pillaging, and so literary influence is a good deal more difficult to gauge. It is in this sense an intimate part of the creative process, and one can usually say little with certainty, without being a rather intimate friend of the writer involved. Not always even then.

Let me illustrate by a personal instance. The Irish playwright John O'Donovan is a considerable authority on Bernard Shaw. He has written an excellent book about Vandaleur Lee's influence on Shaw, entitled *Shaw and the Charlatan Genius.* He has written a play, produced by the Abbey Theatre, entitled *The Shaws of Synge Street,* which is an effective dramatization of the lives of Shaw's family and its friends. He once collaborated in a dramatization of Shaw's novel, *The Irrational Knot.* His personal collection of Shavian materials is better than that of many libraries. He has been, like Shaw, a music critic. He is, as was Shaw, a teetotaller and a vegetarian, and his handwriting even resembles Shaw's. If ever knowledge of and admiration for another writer should have caused literary influence, it should be found in O'Donovan's work. Nevertheless, when reading O'Donovan's plays, one is struck much more by the differences from, rather than the resemblances to Shaw; and I would be quite at a loss in trying to isolate from any single facet of O'Donovan's work that which is indubitably Shavian in its inspiration.

There are, then, difficulties in ascertaining what Irish playwrights have been influenced by Synge and how they have been influenced. Perhaps the safest way to proceed would be to list the notable Syngean characteristics and then to point out where similar characteristics occur in the works of later men.

To me, the most prominent qualities of Synge's plays are the nature of his language and the grotesquerie of his most memorable incidents.

The most individual of Irish playwrights — Synge, Yeats, Lady Gregory, George Fitzmaurice, Sean O'Casey, M. J. Molloy, Brendan Behan, Samuel Beckett — have always been recognizable by the inimitable quality of their dialogue. More ink has probably been spilled in analyzing the rich and individual speech of Synge's people than in evaluating any of his other characteristics. Yet one quality which Synge's dialogue shares with that of Yeats, Lady Gregory and the others is that it is not really useful to another writer.

The reason, I think, is that its finest quality lies in the startling juxtaposition of alien words to produce the most vivid images. This quality arises from Synge's particular genius, his own quite individual way of regarding the world, and is therefore really impossible to imitate. Take this quality away from the other main characteristics of Syngean dialogue — the more noticeable turns of speech and quirks of phrase and heavy rhythms — and there remains only the mannerism and not the soul. Of course, mannerism can be put to some limited use by other writers in the form of parody, and Synge's manner has been sometimes so used with good effect. Gerald Mac-Namara was parodying Synge, among others, in his still un-published *The Mist That Does Be on the Bog.* Denis Johnston parodied Synge, among others, in *The Old Lady Says 'No!'* O'Casey parodied him a bit in *Purple Dust*. Maurice Meldon parodied him in some passages of *Aisling*. But parody has a limited utility, and I think that Synge's language has been most influential not as a specific model, but as a general example of the vividness and richness towards which stage dialogue may aspire.

(To intrude a personal note — James Douglas and I spent several futile years working on a trilogy of plays about types of Irish writers. One play was a Syngean type, one an O'Caseyan and one a Yeatsian. In each play, we wanted to include a half parody-half pastiche of the original author's style. We found, curiously, that Yeats's style was easy to do, that O'Casey's was very easy and that Synge's was well-nigh impossible. We spent much more time analysing Synge's style and certainly knew what had to be done, but the doing was incredibly hard; and we wound up with something which would sound authentic enough if spoken by good actors, but which had an essential tinniness that was quite apparent when one had the leisure to scan it on the page.)

The original antipathy toward Synge was probably so marked because the richness of his language and the grotesquerie of his incidents seemed to intensify his views. As Yeats pointed out, the work of William Boyle was sometimes as caustic in its attitudes, but Boyle's language was much blander and his incidents much less strikingly extravagant.

This extravagant grotesquerie in the situations of *The Shadow of the Glen,* in the last act of *The Well of the Saints,* and throughout *The Playboy* is a trademark of Synge, but it is also apparent in other Irish dramatists who preceded and followed him. In general, I have in mind the lack of reverence for basic social institutions such as the family and the church, and also a rather insouciant view about the value of life. This may sound heretical, but consider, for instance, Synge's corpses. There is the real corpse in *Riders to the Sea* and the businesslike way in which it is treated, and there is the pseudo-corpse of Dan Burke in *The Shadow of the Glen* and the casual way in which it is treated. There is also Nora's desertion at the end of the same play, a desertion which is more shattering to custom and more final than the desertion of Ibsen's more famous Nora at the end of *A Doll's House.* There are so many many obvious and often discussed incidents and attitudes of this nature in *The Playboy,* that perhaps it is enough to note that the voice of convention is given to the gormless and cowardly Shawn Keogh, who is a figure of fun largely because he does acquiesce to convention.

There is something of this same irreverence in quite a few other Irish dramatists, some of whom were far from being social critics.

Dion Boucicault for most of his long and successful career was a crowd-pleasing hack who intended to offend no portion of his audience. Nevertheless, the heroes of his three best known Irish plays are disreputable rascals who gaily drink, poach, steal and swagger through their plays, ignoring convention and delighting in their playboy freedom.

Similarly, Synge's corpses pop up, literally and figuratively, elsewhere, and often in a whimsical or farcical context. In Boucicault's *The Shaughraun,* which Synge may have seen, the most drolly effective scene is the wake in which the indomitable Conn unexpectedly revives and wryly surveys his obsequies. In *The Racing Lug* of 1902, James H. Cousins fore-shadowed Synge's similar treatment of a similar situation in *Riders to the Sea* by two years. In addition to several poetic plays on Irish mythology, Cousins also wrote a full length realistic comedy of Ulster life, entitled *Sold.* Although W. B. Yeats used his influence to prevent the Fays from producing *Sold,* it is not quite the terrible play that Yeats thought. It does tail off badly after a good opening act, but in that act a main character pretends to be dead, and this pseudo-death impels the whole plot.

The same situation appeared years later in M. J. Molloy's vehicle for Siobhan McKenna, *Daughter from over the Water,* when again the man of the house plays dead to stave off his creditors. In both plays, the pseudo-corpse is quickly forgotten by people eager to woo the 'widow', but an even more grotesque situation occurs in Molloy's masterly one-act *The Paddy Pedlar,* in which the Pedlar is carrying the body of his mother around in a sack.

There are enough other such instances to make one ponder. It is easy to cry Syngean influence, but it is also possible to wonder if this grotesque fun and this casualness about life may have appeared so frequently in Irish literature because of certain centuries-long conditions of Irish life. Oppression, rebellion, grinding poverty and unimaginable famine made life so cheap that the only way finally to regard it may have been through the joke. And because a vital matter is treated casually, a sober matter flippantly, the effect is terrifically grotesque. In contrast, sex in Ireland has been dear rather than cheap, and the treatment of sex in Irish literature has until lately been predominantly romantic or tragic. But, at any rate, it is often difficult to say whether this grotesquerie so frequently found in Irish playwrights is a direct influence of Synge or simply an inevitable effect of Irish history.

III

Undoubtedly one can discern some influence of Synge on his friend John Masefield's 1908 play, *The Tragedy of Nan,* and one must surely note D. H. Lawrence's *The Widowing of Mrs Holroyd* and also Paul Green's 1927 attempt in *The Last of the Lowries* to write an American folk play based on the pattern of *Riders to the Sea.* Beyond this, attribution becomes a bit tenuous.

Nevertheless, it seems plausible to suggest that Synge's first major influence was upon the early work of George Fitzmaurice, the eccentric Kerryman whose plays were shamefully neglected during his lifetime, and whose reputation since his death in 1963 has grown almost to rival Synge's own. Still, it is somewhat misleading to compare the two writers, for Fitzmaurice's best work usually has a strong element of the fantastic, which is largely lacking in Synge. It would probably be just to say that Fitzmaurice took the folk play, as practised by Synge, Hyde and Lady Gregory, and so suffused it with myth, legend and his own quaint and satiric fancies, that the final product, in such pieces as *The King of the Barna Men* and *The Enchanted Land,* resembles a Synge play rewritten by Lewis Carroll collaborating with J. R. R. Tolkien.

In Fitzmaurice's simpler and, usually, earlier work, the similarity to Synge's plays is strongest. *The Toothache,* a one-act which is probably among the very first that Fitzmaurice wrote, is a folk play whose grotesque antics might have been written by Synge himself. The popular comedy, *The Country Dressmaker,* was never considered by Yeats to approach the quality of Synge's work, but even Yeats realized that the play's sardonic view of the Irish was akin to that of *The Playboy.* Indeed, Yeats boasted that the *Dressmaker* would bring more policemen into the theatre than had *The Playboy.* *The Pie Dish* and *The Magic Glasses* were one-acts presented by the Abbey in, respectively, 1908 and 1913; and with another one-act, *The Dandy Dolls,* they form a trilogy of short fantastic masterpieces, fully of vitality, drollery, eccentricity and superb speech. As Austin Clarke remarked:

Following Synge's example of a rich rhythmic speech, Fitzmaurice, as a Kerryman, drew his own from his native country. It has in it the rapid rhythm of Kerry Irish and it seems to catch its pace from those fantastically long place-names which one finds in the 'Kingdom.' Its imagery expresses the blending of reality and legend. Reading *The Dandy Dolls,* I wondered how Lady Gregory and Yeats could have failed to recognise the energy, vehement rhythm and imaginative originality of its two short acts, especially when they had already been pleased by *The Magic Glasses*.[2]

Keerby's magnificient speech which concludes *The Dandy Dolls* is well known, and so to give the flavour of Fitzmaurice's dialogue let me quote from the speeches of Morgan Quille, as he lies on the floor in convulsions in *The Magic Glasses*, reciting the cure for Jaymony Shanahan:

Jaymony, Jaymony Shanahan! Let Jaymony Shanahan drink one wineglassful of the bottle left on the table by one Morgan Quille of Beena- horna — three times a day let him drink one wineglass, in the morning and in the noontime and coming on the fall of night. And the price of that bottle is four-and-six — [PADDEN *fumbles in pocket, hands money to* MAINEEN, *who slips it into* QUILLE'S *hand*] — and at the dawn of day let Jaymony Shanahan hop on one leg and make a bow East and West and North and South, and let him pick fourteen roses and make a garland with ferny leaves and eglantine, and leave it on the thatch. [*Works again in convulsions*] Jaymony, Jaymony Shanahan! Let Jaymony Shanahan go turn the red earth every day will rise over him seven hours between dawn and the time the sun goes down, and in the dusk he'll ramble to the neighbours' houses and discourse on cattle and on crops and all things on the agricultural way. He'll go to market and to fair — take drink — a little — and ketch a woman if he wants to when he is coming home. On the twenty-first day a farmer's daughter is to be made out for Jaymony Shanahan. . . Who is the woman to be made out for Jaymony Shanahan? A lovely woman for a man with four cows, no blemish on her beauty, but a slight impediment in her speech. The birthmarks on her are a pimple under her left ear, three black hairs on her buzzom and one brown. In Beenahorna this damsel does dwell, and on the twenty-first day — if Jaymony obey all the instructions given — one Morgan Quille will bring her to Jaymony Shanahan, and on the twenty-second day he'll be cured for ever and live in the grace of God.[3]

Besides the obvious differences between this dialogue and that of Synge, there is also Fitzmaurice's habit of slipping out of tone, usually for satiric purposes. One sees it here in the line about the price of the bottle or in 'take drink — a little.' This is a quality I think uncharacteristic of Synge. But also Fitzmaurice's whimsical images and details are usually intended to raise a spurt of laughter rather than a smile of delight; and here he possibly goes back beyond Synge, Hyde and Lady Gregory to Boucicault for his inspiration. Nevertheless, before Synge, Hyde and Lady Gregory, dialogue with all of Fitzmaurice's qualities could hardly have been written. Compare, for instance, the fairly conventional dialogue of Fitzmaurice's early

short stories, which were done around the turn of this century, to
the dialogue of the post-1906 plays.[4] The difference is between the
traditional exaggeration and a highly individual one.

From the exaggerations of the popular comic vision, it is not far
to the exaggeration of satire and fantasy. As Fitzmaurice grew older
and further removed from a past that he was not even originally firmly rooted in, the satire and the fantasy came to predominate; and
Ireland was no longer the reason, but the excuse for writing. His
folk plays became less and less the depictions of real-life folk
customs, and more and more the depiction of his own imagination.
The best things in his folk plays are the least realistic, the least
ordinary, his galaxy of quaint, eccentric and mad characters.
Obviously he was having the most fun writing about Jaymony
Shanahan who hides in his loft seeing visions in magic glasses, about
Morgan Quille the quack doctor, about Leum Donoghue the
fanatical pie-dish artist, about Lena Hanrahan the flawed beauty
who wears false teeth, a wig and a wooden leg. And in such later
plays as *The Waves of the Sea, The Linnaun Shee, The Green Stone*
and *The Terrible Baisht,* the Kerry countryside has become
transformed into the landscape of Fitzmaurice's mind.

He did make two attempts in his later writings to deal with urban
life, and to deal with it somewhat realistically. *The Coming of Ewn
Andzale* is, however, his only really tedious play, but *One Evening
Gleam* is a little *tour de force.* It is made up largely of reminiscences
about Dublin life early in the century, and then capped by a bizarrely
startling death. But although Fitzmaurice lived most of his adult life
in Dublin, he lived as a semi-recluse, an outsider who was never really
a part of the city; and his most characteristic and finest work came
out of memory and then finally out of memory transformed by a
most extraordinary make-believe.

If this isolation gave Fitzmaurice his strength as a writer, it also
gave him two weaknesses. His language is generally as Synge would
have wanted it: as ripe as a berry. It is as hypnotically fluent and
as playfully inventive as the Synge of *The Playboy* or the O'Casey
of *Purple Dust.* In the voice of a memorable Kerry actor, such as
Eamon Kelly or Eamon Keane, Fitzmaurice's long fancies are a joy.
Here, for instance, is one of Aeneas Canty's speeches from *The
Ointment Blue:*

A murmuring I hear and a gaping I espy, and I do hear it and I do espy
it. But let not the surprise be taking away the seven senses, petrifying the
perceptions or coagulating the mentality or bamboozling the conceptions:

for marvels will happen and marvels will be, though a golden crown will the victor see. And we continue: brooks run and rivers too; grass grows and so do trees; 'chip' from the cricket and buzz from the bee. [*Loudly, waving his hand.*] Silence! Aeneas has said it and 'tis said; fol-de-rol, fol-de-rol, fol-de-dum, fol-de-doo, fol-de-dee, fol-de-dido![5]

But the long speeches are also a problem in many of the later plays. Despite the playfulness, despite engaging experiments with sound, repetition, malapropisms and different levels of language, many of these speeches are more literary than dramatic. If the speeches are read as portions of a novel in dialogue, they are delightful. If they are read with a theatrical ear, as scripts to be spoken in plays to be staged, they are a bit of a problem. Funny, charming, even marvellous sometimes, but a bit of a problem, nevertheless.

A second symptom of Fitzmaurice's isolation is the frequent laziness of his plot construction. A prime example is the published version of his brilliant *The Enchanted Land.* The first and second acts are loaded down with exposition which could profitably and excellently have been dramatized. Indeed, they cry out to be dramatized. The result is that much of the chat in Act One simply tells us what should have been the dramatized story of Act One. Fitzmaurice has attacked his story at the wrong place and has caused his director a quite unnecessary problem of coping with some resulting dullness.

Generally, of course, dullness is quite the last quality that one associates with Fitzmaurice. In his individual fantasies, he has truly created his own world, just as did Lewis Carroll or James Stephens or Kenneth Grahame. The fantastic was the making of Fitzmaurice as an artist. Fantasy allowed him free play for gaiety and wit, and was a liberating influence. Poorer writers have usually but one tone, one emotional slant, one angle of vision on the world. Fitzmaurice seems to have had three: the grotesque in such early work as *The Magic Glasses* and *The Pie-Dish;* the bleakly glum, in which so many of his plays are concluded with a stoical acceptance of failure or, at best, second-best; and the fantastic which allowed him to palliate the grotesquerie and to alleviate the glumness with fun. There is no one quite like him in Irish literature. Among the early Abbey playwrights, his reputation, much belatedly, is probably second now only to that of Synge. As a first-rate spokesman of the second-best, he probably would have found some dour solace in that. If he had noticed it at all.

Other than Fitzmaurice, the Irish theatre up to the emergence of O'Casey showed little obvious influence of Synge. There were some faintly macabre touches in the minor work of Lennox Robinson, and in Winifred Letts and John Guinan (who once collaborated with Fitzmaurice), but generally this period was dominated by realistic comedy and tragedy, chiefly from Robinson, T. C. Murray, Rutherford Mayne and St. John Ervine. In the 1920s, the example of O'Casey imposed a pattern of heightened realism upon the Irish drama. Later, O'Casey himself was to develop this pattern into a unique kind of pastoral fantasy, but the influential O'Casey remained the one who had written *Juno and the Paycock*. For years this heightened realism held joint sway on the boards with the more prosaic older realism, now best exemplified by the plays of George Shiels, and the mainstream of the Irish drama seemed far distant indeed from the impulse of Synge.

Most of the Irish plays since the second World War show even less overt influence of Synge. Partly, the reason is that Synge's plays were about an unspoiled rural Ireland which has been quickly dying. Of the writers who still actually live in the countryside, who have strong roots there and whose important work reflects the life there, the best are probably Bryan MacMahon, Michael J. Molloy and John B. Keane.

MacMahon, who has been a life-long schoolmaster in Listowel, County Kerry, has one of the most impressive theatrical talents of his generation, although he has not utilized it much. He was born in 1909, and his early work, poems and stories and essays, appeared in Sean O'Faolain's magazine, *The Bell*. MacMahon made his reputation first as a writer of short stories, and his main creative energies have always been directed to fiction. Of his four long plays, the first, *Bugle in the Blood,* is the least important. Although it has its grotesqueries and its melodramatic fight, it is mainly reminiscent of *Juno and the Paycock*. MacMahon's major plays are *Song of the Anvil* and *The Honey Spike*. The first is set in an isolated valley in Kerry where the old ways and traditions linger on, and the play shows how the old ways collide disastrously with the modern world. The story teller, Ulick Madigan, whose tales bring colour and vitality, as well as the interest of the outside world, into the valley, explains the problem well to a reporter from the city:

To you this place is picturesque. To me it's daft and desolate. And it's dying fast. Once, out of the struggle for the land, came the storytellers, dancers, poets, men who made fiddle-music fit to stir the stars. But they are all dead — all dead, I tell you, man. The young people — they have all gone across the sea. We were alone and moving toward our end. And then, when all seemed lost, one winter's night, we held a trial all night long until the crack of dawn to find who'd tell a flamin' variegated lie . . . I won! And do you know what 'twas like? 'Twas like as if the Voice of God was roaring from my blood.[6]

MacMahon in this play suggests that the spirit of the Gaelic past may be combined with the Catholic tradition and even with the spirit of the modern world. But, although he has written a moving and theatrical play slashed through with humour and fantasy and romance and extravagance, he has not, I think, found either an aesthetic formula or a social one to blend the old with the new. This play, for the most part, gets its strength from the past. Despite its young American heroine and despite the reporter, the modern world remains pretty much offstage. The play is something of a fantasy, something more of a wish-fulfilment, than an actuality. It is a lovely wish-fulfilment, of course, and much of its comedy, melodrama and national colour have a distinctly Syngean flavour. In the ferocious ending, for instance, the villagers tie Ulick up and attempt to brand him, as Pegeen Mike and the villagers attempted to do to Christy Mahon. There is a further reminiscence in the vitality and sense of aliveness that the old life brings to MacMahon's people, and it comes from the same source that turned Christy into a playboy.

The Honey Spike is the best play to have been written about the travelling people since Synge's *The Tinker's Wedding*. Like Maurice Walsh, MacMahon knows his tinkers well; he is mentioned, for instance, in Muriel Rukeyser's rather poor book about Puck Fair, *The Orgy*. MacMahon's play, which he later turned into a novel, is a more ambitious work than Synge's, for it is not only a re-creation of the tinker life, but also an odyssey through the length of Ireland. As young Martin Claffey rushes his wife Breda from the Giant's Causeway to the Honey Spike, the hospital in Kerry, where she wants to have her baby, we are really seeing again the clash of the old Ireland with the new. In their travels with pony and cart, the Claffeys meet a cross-section of modern Ireland. The play contains a Syngean abundance of riddles and ballads and fights and violence, and also a death scene of much poignance. I have quoted Martin Claffey's speech on Breda's death in an earlier book, but it seems appropriate to do it here again, in this context where we are stressing speech that is 'as fully flavoured as a nut or apple':

Breda! Breda Claffey! Breda, you lovely bitch that I love as man has never loved a woman before. Breda! Come out and walk with me again. Come out and swing your arms around my neck. You've made no complaint of me. I raced you from the Causeway in the Six. We made the bed of honour

30, 40, 60 times, we did. Come out, let you! For you I raced my cob. Through guns and hurleys lifted above my head I brought you to your honey spike. Come out, I tell you now. Come out! The two of us were grand. Only come out, let you, and then the pony-bells will ring for us again. Hey! Breda Claffey, listen now! Listen, I tell you! The world is thronged with things is lovely at the break o'day. Come out, you stubborn heedless strap! Come out, or else I'll drag you by your hair. I tell you that I'll drag you by your. . . lovely shining rippling hair.[7]

If one were listing ten great speeches from the Irish drama, I suppose one must start with Synge's Maurya and O'Casey's Juno, but somewhere in the list must come Martin Claffey's lament for his wife Breda.

MacMahon and Michael J. Molloy a few years ago were somewhere in the wilds of Canada, trying to get a plane back to Shannon and having lost their luggage. MacMahon phoned up the Aer Lingus office, gave their names and explained their problem, and the girl answered. 'Don't worry. We wouldn't take off without *The Honey Spike* and *The King of Friday's Men.*'

Michael J. Molloy, who wrote *The King of Friday's Men,* is the only writer of his generation who has written dramatic speech of an eloquence to equal MacMahon's. And I think he has written more such speeches, for he has written more plays. Indeed, unlike Mac-Mahon, he has so far devoted himself entirely to plays.

Molloy was born in 1917 in Co. Galway where his father was a shopkeeper and his mother a national schoolteacher, and where he now owns a farm. His plays tend to be either historical dramas, like his masterly *The King of Friday's Men,* or comic dramas of the present day which depict the depopulation of the West. Yet 'comic dramas' is a misleading term for plays like *The Visiting House, The Wood of the Whispering* and *Old Road.* Such pieces contain elements of comedy and deeply felt seriousness as well as much farce and melodrama and romance, but the unifying quality is a pervasive and brooding melancholy over the passing of a civilisation that until recently had remained essentially unchanged for centuries.

Molloy is steeped in the traditions, the history, the myths and the folklore of the West. What Synge acquired by persistent inquiry, Molloy obtained by simply living in a certain place for all of his life. It is, then, difficult to say what precisely Molloy owes to Synge and what he owes merely to treating a similar subject-matter. Certainly the resemblances between their work, and even its manner, are striking. Molloy, as was Synge, is a slow writer and a meticulous reviser. Much that goes into his plays is built up of incidents and anecdotes and turns of speech, remembered and jotted down from first-hand observation. Much of this has an authentic and arresting piquancy about it. In some ways, Molloy seems a more authentic Synge, a Synge sitting on a settle in the kitchen rather than listening through a chink in the bedroom floor. Molloy's dialogue is closer to the way people talked, while Synge's dialogue is an embroidery, a dramatization, a heightening. Elsewhere I have suggested that Molloy's dialogue lies about midway between that of George Shiels, which represents a thinning of language, and that of Synge, which represents a thickening of it. Each has its excellences and its drawbacks. Synge's dialogue has much of the evocative power of poetry, while Shiels's has practically none; Synge's dialogue offers distinct problems as stage speech, while Shiels's has an easy fluency and sometimes even a savage force. Molloy's dialogue is a kind of compromise which poses some difficulties as stage speech, and which yet retains much evocative power. There are rhythms in Molloy's long speeches which amplify the emotional power, but the rhythms are less obtrusive than the Syngean ones. There is also a less imaginative use of metaphor and figure in Molloy than in Synge, although there is some; the principal evocative power of Molloy's dialogue comes, I think, from his diction which is, for the most part, unfamiliar without being baffling, and fresh enough to be engaging. Some of Molloy's best effects come from a quiet mournfulness, such as the beautiful speech of the old man, Mickle Conlon, which concludes *The Visiting House,* or several speeches of Sanbatch Daly to Sadie the mute in *The Wood of the Whispering,* or Biddy the Tosser's speech which concludes his recent play *Petticoat Loose.* Mickle's speech is long, and yet this ambling monologue, delivered by the old man after everyone unbeknownst to him has left the stage, is such an exquisite dying fall, and such a perfect parallel to the gentle fading away of Mickle's world, that I cannot resist giving it in full:

And now, Corry, wance you behaved such a decent man, I'll give you good advices that'll stand to you well when you're going dying, the same as me now. Your first plan, then, asthore, 'll be to coax the Mother of God, for she has a great hand with Our Saviour, and anything she wants she has only to ask Him. Wan single falling out! − that was all they had in all their time together on earth, and there wasn't much to that; there was not, asthore. They were going the road this day, asthore, and they seen a fellow that was someway crippled, and out of his proper shape. 'Son,' she sez, 'you made a poor job of that wan' − she didn't think of herself; she did not, asthore. Our Saviour said no word till duskus, then, 'Mother,' he said, 'in place of you and Me stopping in the wan lodging house tonight, I'll stop in the first house on the right, and you in the first house on the left.' So they did,

asthore, and she went in, and found a corpse laid overboard on the Kitchen
table, and snuff and tobaccy, and a gross of pipes and all ready for the
wake, asthore. So, the same as everywan had to do before your time, she
took a pipe and said, 'The Lord have mercy on the dead!' and she smoked
away there in honour of the dead; but not a single person come in to the
wake, asthore, and she was by herself with the corpse till the morning. That
was the penance Our Saviour put on her, so He must be middling vexed
to her that day, all right. But that finished that, and 'twas the only falling
out they had ever, asthore. Anything she wants she has only to ask Him,
so keep her on your side, and when your tenure of time is up 'tis she'll have
your bed dressed in Heaven and the finest of welcomes before
you. [*Wandering.*] That's sure, asthore, that's sure, asthore . . . [*Suddenly
and sternly.*] Corry, did you let that advice to you? [*Thundering.*] Corry,
answer up and don't be disorderly. Corry! [*Finally he pokes out his stick,
finds the form empty, and smiles.*] He's at large; he is, asthore. [*Turns
back to fire cheerfully.*] No matter; now you'll have two half barrels, and
the finest wake since the time of the gentleman; now you can die away for
yourself, asthore . . . [*Gravely.*] For the first while right enough you'll be
lonesome for the village; and lonesome for the Visiting House, too.
[*Nodding.*] You will, in throth, asthore. . . But wance you have the
lonesomeness and your Purgatory over, you'll be all right? [*In great
humour.*] you'll be as snug as a lamb in a shed; you will, asthore . . . asthore
. . .[8]

This is a characteristic passage of Molloy, deep in feeling and melancholy in tone. Its resemblances to and its differences from Synge
are probably apparent without comment. What is curious, though,
is that Molloy can counterpoint such passages with ones of vigour
and violence. And it is violence not only of language, but of action.
Like Synge and Fitzmaurice, Molloy is fond of the stage fight, and
there are finely melodramatic ones in *Old Road,* in *The King of Friday's Men* and in that macabre little masterpiece, *The Paddy Pedlar.*
'Hullabaloo! Hullabaloo!' cries Molloy's pedlar:

[*Twice he leaps into the air with that hiss of savage joy; drawing back the
knife each time as if about to charge at Ooshla. But instead he leaps again,
and cries aloud in triumph.*] Now, Mamma! Timmy has his knife! Timmy
has his knife! Timmy has his knife! No one'll dare harm you no more![9]

But perhaps the greatest similarity between Synge and Molloy is that
their worlds are both peopled by outcasts and eccentrics. Molloy's
is a world of sad, lonely people, pushed into weirdness or quaint-
ness or wildness or madness. His Bully Men and Bards and Mutes
and Pedlars are as outcast as Synge's Tramps and Tinkers and
Playboys and Blind Men. The one great difference between Molloy's
characters and Synge's is that Synge's usually triumph over their

circumstances, while Molloy's are usually defeated. Molloy is a muted Synge, more sad than bitter, more musing than lyrical, and that perhaps is appropriate because the world they both wrote of is fading.

John B. Keane is probably the most recent writer whose work might seem akin to Synge's. He has been a prolific playwright, and would be mentioned with Brian Friel and Hugh Leonard as one of the important playwrights of the last twenty years. As with Molloy, whose influence he admits, Keane has never really left Ireland. In his youth he was, like many other young Irishmen, forced to emigrate to England, but this short exile he resented bitterly, and his play about the subject, *Hut 42,* is a poignant lament of the exile for his homeland. Most of Keane's plays reflect the life he intimately knows in the Southwest of Ireland. Once I argued that this was still a kind of Hidden Ireland, with a life richer and larger and more basically Irish than life in the modern Dublin of television antennas, exhaust fumes and rectangular office slabs of concrete and glass. That was probably only half-true when I wrote it, and even less true now. Tourism has become a highly organized and profitable business, and the Irish Tourist Board is industriously tempting hordes of Americans and English to explore the remarkable beauties of the Irish countryside. This influx of people and money has combined with the impact of the modern world as seen through television, to effect considerable change in the West and the South. So while the earlier Keane plays resembled Syngean folk plays about the traditional past, his later work — such as *The Field* and *Big Maggie* and *The Good Thing* — reflects a clash of an older way of life with a new.

The Keane plays which are most Syngean are his first three — *Sive, Sharon's Grave* and *The Highest House on the Mountain.* In these folk plays, the most prominent reminiscences of Synge are a sardonic grotesquerie of characterization and action, as well as some richness in the language. Characters such as the matchmaker and the travelling tinkers in *Sive,* such as Dinzie Conlee, the savage and sex-crazed hunchback in *Sharon's Grave,* came down from the mountains out of the same mist and rain as did Synge's Michael Casey and Old Mahon fifty years earlier.

There is also much Syngean violence in these early plays. As Martin Doul strikes the can of holy water from the hand of the Saint, as the Caseys truss up the priest and throw him into the ditch, as Christy cleaves his father's head with the loy, and Pegeen Mike burns Christy's leg with the turf, so also is Keane's world a violent one. There is especially that harrowing scene at the conclusion of *Sharon's Grave,* which begins when Dinzie Conlee cries, 'I'll lop this knife between the beasts of her and stick her like a pig,' and then crawls across the floor after his cousin Trassie; and which concludes when Neelus, the simpleton, races out with the hunchback on his own back to plunge over the cliff into the sea.

Keane's dialogue has sometimes been admired for its force, but in these early folk plays it also has a richness which is less embroidered than Synge's, but still reminiscent of it. Here, for instance, is Tomasheen Sean Rua in *Sive* speaking to Mike Glavin and his wife Meana:

Will you listen to him! You're like the priest in the pulpit! Will you think of the days of your life you spent slavin' for nothin'. You needn't rise off your bottom to earn two hundred sovereigns, and you sit there giving sermons! And you talk about love! In the name of God, what do the likes of us know about love? Did you ever hear the word of love on his lips? Ah, you did not, girl! Did he ever give you a little rub behind the ear or run his fingers through your hair and tell you he would swim the Shannon for you? Did he ever sing the love-songs for you in the far-out part of the night when ye do be alone? He would sooner to stick his snout in a plate of mate and cabbage, or to rub the back of a fattening pig than whisper a bot of his fondness for you. Do he run to you when he come in from the bog and put his arms around you and give you a big smohawnach of a kiss and tell you that the length of the day was like the length of a million years while he was separated from you?[10]

This dialogue lacks the more obvious Syngean characteristics of lengthy sentences and thickly rhythmical speech, but there is some of the same quality in the diction and in the nature of the imagery and certainly in the vitality that pervades it. And perhaps there is also a more obvious emotion, for in some parts of Synge the language does clog up the emotion a bit.

In the Preface to the *The Playboy,* Synge wrote of 'countries where the imagination of the people, and the language they use, is rich and living.' He spoke of 'the wildest sayings and ideas', of 'the rich joy found only in what is superb and wild in reality', of speech that is 'fully flavoured as a nut or apple'. To us who have come with delight upon these rare qualities in the plays of John Synge, it is an appalling loss that the world from which these qualities rose, the world of which Synge was one of the best interpreters, is passing. The playwrights I have mentioned all live in a world which Synge never dreamed of, and their plays either transmute that old Ireland into fantasy or show it grappling, sometimes successfully but more often not, with the modern world. I think that the playwrights to come will not for much longer be able to write plays like Molloy's or MacMahon's or the early ones of Keane − and yet it is possible that the qualities which Synge most valued in his country, joy and richness, may take some new form which is both modern and Irish. In the 1920s, Sean O'Casey found joy and richness in the world of the Dublin slums, and in the 1940s and 1950s he found another new way to write with joy and richness of the modern world. In the 1950s Brendan Behan found a way. So perhaps it does not matter if Synge's manner be lost; those who were most influenced by him never attempted to imitate it, but only to emulate it, to sieve its spirit through their own individualities. A Brian Friel, a Hugh Leonard, a James Douglas, a Heno Magee may yet find a new way for a new time. It is only the richness and joy that matter, and in those qualities Synge has given his real legacy to the men who came after.

THERE IS REALISM AND REALISM

It must have been Ernest A. Boyd, in his fine 1917 volume *The Contemporary Drama of Ireland,* who first formulated one of the major ways in which we have since thought about the Irish drama. In the beginning, said Boyd – that is, as early as the Irish Literary Theatre of 1899 – there were two dramatic impulses at work. One was the poetic drama of W. B. Yeats, and the other was the realistic drama of Edward Martyn. And, so the argument goes, even though Martyn left the Abbey movement, realism did not. Indeed, the first really successful full-length Abbey play was William Boyle's realistic study of grasping peasants, *The Building Fund.* Yeats, of course, was the dominant personality and the unchallenged leader of the Abbey Theatre, but his army formed up behind Boyle, who was waving Martyn's flag, and marched off in another direction. Thus, the Abbey, which was intended as a poet's theatre, became a theatre of prose realists. And, concluded Boyd, it would not be until these two divergent streams re-united that the dramatic movement would fully flourish.

There is some truth in this simple formulation, especially if we take the terms loosely: if under Poetry, we rank Lyricism, Fantasy, Music, Dance and Experimentation; if under Prose, we rank Irony, Realism, Comedy, Tragedy and Traditionalism. And, of course, if we keep our notions of categories loose, and allow that brilliant writers have always merged genres, melded forms and generally played fast and loose with the tidy schematics of academe.

There is some truth – but far from the whole truth. For one thing, Yeats considerably encouraged many of the most realistic playwrights, such as R. J. Ray, and highly lauded others, such as T. C. Murray. The early Abbey hand-out, 'Advice to Playwrights,' was most certainly drafted by Yeats and Lady Gregory, and was a document full of elementary commonsense about realistic playwriting. Also, Yeats's closest colleagues, Synge and Lady Gregory, had each a foot firmly in the realistic camp. Synge's song, as well as his grotesquerie, made him seem unrealistic, or even a perversion of realism; Lady Gregory's Kiltartan, as well as her exaggerated comedy, made her seem unrealistic, or even a parody of realism. But, in their dramatic practice, both were as close to Boyle as to Yeats.

Another falsity in Boyd's formulation is in seeing Edward Martyn as the father of the realistic impulse. He was not. A good deal of ink has been spilled over the plays of Edward Martyn, and I do not intend to add appreciably to it. Martyn's plays have no standing as literature, and the original theatrical impact of *The Heather Field* has faded with the historical and political reasons for it. Cornelius Weygandt years ago, in a gentle but just discussion, isolated Martyn's overwhelming dramatic fault, the thorough awkwardness of his dialogue.[1] This stiltedness pervades and debilitates every play that Martyn wrote. Una Ellis-Fermor professed to see a distinct difference in the quality of *The Heather Field* and that of the later *The Tale of a Town*.[2] Such a difference quite eludes me, to whom both seem almost equally dreadful.[3]

The reasons for Martyn's awkwardness seem traceable to certain qualities of character — his early introspection and diffidence, and his later eccentricity and religiosity. And to the fact that he never worked at his writing. It was something that he did sporadically, and so he remained an amateur of letters, of only historical importance.

The cliché about Martyn's plays, derived from *The Heather Field* and the Martyn-Moore *Bending of the Bough,* is that Martyn was a disciple of Ibsen, writing realistic or satiric social dramas about such phlegmatic subjects as agricultural reform. If so, Martyn's plays would be a neat counter-balance to those of Yeats: the realistic, continentally influenced social criticism of the present vs. the romantic, poetic celebration of the Irish peasant and the mythical Irish past. In actuality, *The Heather Field, Maeve* and *The Bending of the Bough* are romantic, symbolic and, in a broad sense, poetic. If Martyn owed a debt to Ibsen, it was not to the Ibsen of *An Enemy of the People,* but to the Ibsen of *The Lady from the Sea.*

Still another falsity in Boyd's formulation is the implication that there is just one brand of realism, and it a kind of photographic, Zolaesque, slice-of-life reportage. Not so. There is realism and realism; and it is probably only the succession of pale neo-Galsworthian imitations of Ibsen, that has convinced us that realism is uniform, and that prose is prosaic.

Let me arbitrarily distinguish several kinds of realistic writers (and this is indeed arbitrary because, although hack writers always write in the same way, good writers write with different manners, modes and intentions from play to play).

First, there is the photographic realist, of whom I can think of no outstanding examples among the Irish. Perhaps to an extent George Shiels in his wry later plays comes fairly close, as does also St. John Ervine who is, however, a bit too selective and caustic to be an accurate example. Or perhaps Heno Magee or the Sheridan brothers in the present. A good foreign example might be Hauptmann in *The Weavers,* or Elmer Rice in *Street Scene.* A bad Irish example would be Sean O'Casey who was initially labelled a photographic realist. Gabriel Fallon has described how O'Casey listened avidly for turns of phrase as he walked the streets of Dublin, but O'Casey was not listening as a Zola-like tape recorder.[4] He was listening for the exciting phrase, the moving one, the witty one, the exaggerated conceit, and he threw them in profusion into his plays. In fact, they occurred more profusely in his early plays than they did in life. O'Casey chose the raciest of what people said; a photographic realist chooses whatever people say, whether it be witty or boring. Such a writer is the naturalist of the drama, the inheritor of the mantle of Zola. He uses words for their reality to a real-life situation rather than for their dramatic effect.

Second, there is the prosaic realist who is as devoted to the actuality of what people say as is the photographic realist, but who is a good deal more selective in dialogue and manipulative in plot. Among the Irish, the prime example is probably T. C. Murray. Murray achieved his effects by a meticulous plotting and a gradual accretion of detail. Ibsen of the middle period was Murray's master. In the best of Murray, as in Ibsen, there is great strength in the slow, cumulative movement that finally bursts forth in an impetuous rush of climactic action. However, a lesser Ibsen like Murray also runs the risk of dullness, particularly in the early passages of a play. The chief antidotes that a prosaic realist has against dullness are the terse and impeccable exactness of his dialogue and also an occasional level of irony above the primary meaning of his words.

Irony is probably the chief rhetorical device of the satiric realist, and he uses irony much more frequently than the prosaic realist (and, of course, the photographic realist would hardly use irony at all). If the photographic realist writes to expose reality without comment, and the prosaic realist writes finally to comment on what he has exposed, the satiric realist writes to comment critically. Among the earlier Irish playwrights, Lennox Robinson occasionally wrote satirically, and Gerald MacNamara practically always did. Among the middle playwrights, there is a good deal of satirical realism in Mary Manning, Lady Longford and sometimes Louis D'Alton. Among the recent playwrights, Brian Friel in an occasional play like

The Mundy Scheme is a satirical realist, and so certainly is Michael Judge in the delightful prologue to his *Saturday Night Women*. The satirical realist would choose his words primarily for their ironic effect. Unlike his brother realists, he would either exaggerate the faults of ordinary discourse or would frequently choose its more absurd specimens. The dialogue of some of Mervyn Wall's novels or of much of his play *Alarm among the Clerks* is often satirical. In American writing, the Sinclair Lewis of *Main Street* and *Babbitt* would be a prime example, and so also would most of Ring Lardner.

Perhaps a comic realism ought to be mentioned. Lennox Robinson's best plays are probably his genial comedies, particularly *The White-headed Boy* and *The Far Off Hills,* in which he is trying to expose foibles more than to lash faults. In such pieces, the dialogue is true, a bit discursive, and funny without being exaggerated or heightened. Wit and fancy have but small part in it, as wit and fancy have but small part in real discourse. Such dialogue has a deceptive fluency, for it pleases without drawing attention to itself, and it charms almost subliminally. The dialogue of O'Casey's early Dublin plays is probably at the very outer edge of comic realism. O'Casey's dialogue is rooted in reality, but, as with Dickens' dialogue, there is an inordinate profusion of roots. O'Casey's dialogue is usually much funnier than Robinson's, as Dickens's dialogue is usually much funnier than Jane Austen's; but it is so funny that it calls attention to why it is funny. This, of course, is not to say that O'Casey's early dialogue is bad; it is generally accepted as some of the best comic dialogue of the modern drama. It is also, though, a bit more comic than realistic.

Finally one might mention a poetic realism which strikes me as the hardest to spot, the hardest to discuss and the hardest to write. By poetic realism, I mean a style which is basically plausible on the stage as true speech, but which has embedded throughout words and phrases so aptly and yet freshly chosen that they make the surrounding ordinary words come alive also with an unusual and evocative vigor. I am not speaking of bejewelled prose or purple passages, but of a prose that never sinks below a level of luminous clarity, and that sometimes rises to eloquence. Maurya's final speeches in Synges's most austerely written play, *Riders to the Sea,* are probably the touchstone; but there is much also to be found in the early plays of Padraic Colum. Such dialogue is still definitely, sturdily realistic, but its words are chosen with the hard eye of the poet. The most difficult effect to achieve in any literary genre is eloquence, and the rare eloquence of poetic realism has given us some of the least gaudy, yet most moving passages in the modern drama.

II

There is no end to making categories, and the ones above may be possibly not the best ones to have set up, but they do show, I think, that the house of realism has many mansions. Rather than be too pedantic and try to give pure examples of each category, let me instead investigate the work of some early realists who wrote in various realistic manners. I will confine myself to earlier writers rather than those of the present day because the unobtrusive accomplishment of the past is often forgotten. So let us consider the texture of some early writing which has never received the ferocious scrutiny afforded the work of Yeats and Synge.

First of all, realistic writing of any kind is not like this:

TYRRELL. [*Turns, surprised*]. Miss Desmond − Oh − [*With emotion and signs of struggle.*] Oh, where is that beauty now − that music of the morning? [*Suddenly arrested.*] Such strange solemn harmonies. [*Listens.*] The voices − yes, they are filling the house − those white-stoled children of the morning. [*His eyes after a moment wander slowly to the doorway at back.*] Oh, the rainbow! [*To Kit.*] Come quick, see the lovely rainbow! [*They go to watch it hand in hand.*] Oh, mystic highway of man's speechless longings! My heart goes forth upon the rainbow to that horizon of joy! [*With a fearful exaltation.*] The voices − I hear them now triumphant in a silver glory of song![5]

That was the protagonist's final speech in Edward Martyn's *The Heather Field*, and it is neither realistic nor good. Martyn's writing fails because it is overwritten and theatrical; here is an example which is underwritten and theatrical:

WIDOW. Don't, Mike, don't . . . for the love o'heaven!
MIKE. [*Throwing his mother roughly aside*] : By God! I'll make you suffer for your treachery!
HUGH. [*Trying to avoid onslaught*]: Stop, Mike, stop!
MIKE. [*In a frenzy of blind rage*]: Take that! [*He strikes his step-brother full on the forehead with the poker.*]
[*Hugh staggers and drops to the ground. The Sergeant has sprung forward but is too late to prevent the murderous blow. Mike, panting, gazes at the fallen figure.*].
WIDOW. [*Nearly hysterical*]: Oh, God! Mike, what have you done? You've killed him. [*She kneels down by Hugh's side and tries to lift his head.*] Look up, Hugh, look up. . . . It's not dead you are . . . speak!
[*The Sergeant kneels down and examines the stricken man.*]

SERGEANT. [*Looking up startled*]: Good God! He's dead![6]

This is from the concluding scene of J. Bernard MacCarthy's tragedy *Kinship*. Although the dialogue is much truer than Martyn's, it is so terse that it is little more than annotation for actors. Possibly in a good production, this scene might be carried off. That is, it might work as theatre although it has no standing as dramatic literature. But if it works as theatre, it nevertheless fails as realistic tragedy. It is underwritten into melodrama, and melodrama is not realism.

III

William Boyle is not worth writing much about because, despite his twenty years of popularity, his each succeeding play declined in quality. His first success and quite his best play is *The Building Fund*. This was a play which Yeats regarded with some puzzlement, for it seemed quite as critical of the Irish as did the *Playboy,* and yet audiences were delighted by *The Building Fund* for years. The very disparate reaction to the two plays arose partly, I think, because Boyle's awful misers lived in a sane, kind and admirable world; but they were unique in it. Synge's people were all grotesques and so, therefore, the whole world that he painted was grotesque. Boyle's grotesques were only particular individuals in Ireland; Synge's were the Irish.

Perhaps another reason for the disparate reactions was that Boyle wrote what we might call prosaic realism, and Synge wrote an extravagant prose-poetry with some roots in Irish. Synge's style in *The Playboy* is, of course, one of the triumphs of modern dramatic writing, a rich and inimitable touchstone. But Boyle's unobtrusive method has its own excellences. Prosaic realism is probably an unfortunate term, for it suggests a dullness and stolidity that its best examples entirely lack. Here, as one best example, is a scene from the first act of *The Building Fund:*

[*O'Callaghan and MacSweeney come in from yard. The latter carries a collecting-book in his hand.*]
O'CALLAGHAN. We might be rapping at the front door till Sunday.
MacSWEENEY. That's the only day the miserable creatures open it.
O'CALLAGHAN. They'll have to open it wide enough before long to let out the old woman's coffin. God knows she might grow a little tender at the end of her days, but it's harder and harder she gets. Still, she's decency, itself, compared with her son.

MacSWEENEY. Well, if they don't open their purse for the Building Fund, Father Andrew will read them out the Riot Act.

O'CALLAGHAN. And why wouldn't he? [*Knocks on table.*] The Grogans must behave like other people. Everyone subscribes but them. If they won't, they should be made examples of. [*Knocks again.*]

MacSWEENEY. Shan's coming at last. When he finds he can't shut the door in our faces, he'll try to put us off with blarney.

[*Grogan comes in.*]

GROGAN. Boys, O boys! Is it yourselves that's in it? It's a cure for sore eyes to see the pair of you. Won't ye take the weight off your limbs, gentlemen? Come over here to the fire. Sorrow be off that lazy girl, she let it out again! Never mind. It's the fine, warm weather that's in it, glory be to God! only a little showery for the haymaking. And how is all your care, Mr. O'Callaghan? I was sorry to the heart to hear about the loss of your poor Aunt Ellen. I wouldn't have missed the funeral on any account, only the mare had such a bad cough on my hands.

[*They remain standing.*]

O'CALLAGHAN. We call, Mr. Grogan, regarding the collection for the new church. Father Andrew hopes you'll give us something towards the building fund.[7]

This deft, little scene has an extraordinary economy. As it occurs at the very beginning of the play, it must give some exposition about the miserly old Mrs. Grogan and about her even more miserly son, and it also immediately plunges us into a fine comic situation. The language of the visitors is simply true, terse and realistic, but the speech of Grogan is a superb use of blarneying clichés which both the visitors and the audience see through as utter hypocrisy. What Grogan says could, in other contexts, be said sincerely, and yet the words are so justly chosen that everyone sees through them. We even see through the red herrings of the lazy girl who allegedly let the fire go out, and of the assumed concern for the death of Aunt Ellen, and of the spurious excuse for Shan's not attending the funeral. Boyle has not been revived for years and was never taken with great seriousness by the critics. In part, the fault for the decline of his reputation was his own, for he became an ever broader writer; but in this scene — and, indeed, in this whole play — he beautifully exemplifies the subtleties and nuances that a realistic, prosaic dialogue can accomplish.

Boyle's most popular play was *The Eloquent Dempsy* which Arthur Sinclair played hundreds of times. It is a comedy which slides toward farce, but which is held back by the realistic quality of the language. In an O'Casey play, most of the characters speak in a noticeably comic manner, with all of the devices of comic rhetoric such as non-sequiturs, malapropisms, tag-lines and jargon. In the comic realism of Boyle, practically all of the characters but one speak quite normally. In *Dempsy,* only the blowhard protagonist speaks in a heightened manner, and Boyle gets considerable comic distance by juxtaposing Dempsy's inflated platform manner against ordinary speech. For instance:

DEMPSY. I thank my friend in the crowd for his enlivening remark. I am
   well — quite well. The medicine of your approval cures me. The sound
   of your cheers, the vision of your honest faces, the might, the strength,
   the magnitude of this colossal meeting pours new life into my wasted
   frame. An hour ago I lay heart-shaken with despair —
MRS. DEMPSY [*Aside*]. May the Lord forgive you![8]

There are many such examples in the play. None has the droll fancy of an O'Casey line, but most are unspectacularly effective. By writing most of his comedy simply, Boyle provided a believable landscape. Dempsy stands in bold relief against that landscape, but it is the landscape that keeps him from being transformed into the Wizard of Oz or an Irish W. C. Fields.

In comparing Boyle's dialogue to Synge's and O'Casey's, we must admit that theirs is infinitely finer. Theirs is also extravagant; and, if we are committed to reality as well as to extravaganza in art, then we must also admit that Boyle unobtrusively and successfully went about his business.

IV

In April, 1910, Padraic Colum wrote a short introduction for his play, *Thomas Muskerry,* in which he made some interesting statements about it and his previous plays, *The Land* and *The Fiddler's House*:

The three plays have a theme in common: Murtagh Cosgar, Mary
Hourican, and Thomas Muskerry have each to face a problem arising out
of the life of the family. The father, the daughter, and the grandfather,
are held to the group by something of self-interest: they have put some of
their ambition into the formation or the maintenance of the family, and
each is opposed by one of a like character . . . .
   Some years ago I thought of a grandiose task, the writing of the comedy
of Irish life through all the social stages. I had thought of the work (perhaps
after discovering Balzac) as a piece of social history. I no longer think of

such grandiose plans. But I am glad that I have been able to set down three
characters that stood as first types in my human comedy, the peasant, the
artist, the official; — Murtagh Cosgar, Conn Hourican, Thomas
Muskerry.[9]

It is a great loss to the Irish drama that Colum ceased to think so
grandiosely, for, despite its considerable interest, his later work
remains basically that of a minor writer. And Colum could have been
a great deal more had there been some informing thread holding his
work together. Instead, he wrote in many genres and manners, much
as circumstances or momentary interest dictated — a eulogistic
biography of Griffith who had been his friend and mentor, a memoir
of his friend Joyce, an occasional novel, some commissioned work
on Phillipine Folklore, casual journalism and book reviewing, lyric
poems as the spirit moved him, children's books and travel books
to keep the wolf from the door, and sporadic experiments in various
kinds of unrealistic drama. Without derogating the work of a man
who wrote proficiently and variously through a quite long career,
it seems to me that Colum steadfastly refused to be as great a writer
as he could have been. Perhaps the refusal, if it was a conscious one,
came from the same qualities of character that inform his best work
— simplicity, humility, kindness.

Colum sporadically returned to playwriting. There was *Mogu of
the Desert,* an Arabian romance whose idea Colum always thought
Edward Knoblock had stolen for the successful *Kismet.* Colum's
Eastern idyll was written about 1910 or '11, underwent many
revisions over a period of about twenty years, and was finally published by Macmillan in 1923 and produced by the Gate in 1931 with
the young Orson Welles. There is small possibility of, or reason for,
its revival.

The Grasshopper was produced in New York by Belasco and then
a few years later, in 1922, by the Abbey. It is a very free adaptation
of a European play by Count Keyserling, and is something of a return
to the poetic realism of his Dublin trilogy. Despite its origin and a
weak ending, it is the most effective of Colum's later plays and an
indication that realism was his forte.

Colum wrote the Expressionistic *Balloon* in America and tinkered
with it for many years. Macmillan published a version in 1929; and
about ten years later, according to Harold Clurman, the Group
Theatre tried out a version in a public reading. But more than
twenty years later, Colum was still trying to find a producer for it.
The cast list, however, is two pages long, and there were not enough
counter-balancing merits in the script ever to secure a production.

Towards the end of his life, Colum wrote five short plays about Irish figures — Henry Joy McCracken, Sir William Wilde, Parnell, Casement and Joyce. These he described as being in the manner of the Japanese Noh play, but Colum's Plays for Dancers were no more Noh plays than were those of Yeats. Some of them have been produced or published and contain some good lines and lyrics. See, for example, *Moytura* which the Dolmen Press brought out in 1963, or *Cloughoughter* which was published in the Colum number of *The Journal of Irish Literature* in 1973. Nevertheless, as theatrical works these 'Noh plays' must be judged as flat failures. The one which I have produced, *Moytura,* is dull and pretentious, and has some so garbled lines that the only way to read them is as quickly as possible — a curious fact, indeed, considering that Colum's great strength had always been his limpid lucidity.

These, then, were Colum's chief dramatic works in the more than sixty years of his life that followed the production of *Thomas Muskerry* in 1910. The one semi-success is the poetic realism of *The Grasshopper;* but all of the later plays are so inferior to Muskerry that one can only see Colum's abandonment of dramatic realism as a disastrous mistake.

The Land and *The Fiddler's House* were both sound, good plays; and the last of the trilogy, *Muskerry,* trembles on the edge of greatness. One is justified in thinking of the plays as a trilogy, for several reasons. First, there is, as Colum pointed out, their general similarity as family tragedies in which a particular social issue is fought out in the battleground of the home. This is a traditional and seemingly inevitable form for classic drama — as plays from *Oedipus Rex* to *Hamlet* to *Juno and the Paycock* testify. Second, a basic attitude toward drama permeates the plays. As Colum wrote of them:

The dramatist is concerned not primarily with the creation of character, but with the creation of situations. For character conceived as a psychological synthesis he has only a secondary concern. His main effort is always toward the creation of situations that will produce a powerful impression on an audience, for it is situation that makes the strongest appeal to our sympathies.[10]

This, of course, is the traditional view of what drama has been in the western world; and the first critic to state it was Aristotle. The clarity with which Colum as a very young dramatist repeated the point for himself is a strong sympton of how centrally placed his early plays were in the main tradition of Western drama.

Like all traditional dramatists who recognized the centrality of situation and who were much more than hacks, Colum wrote good characters and even one memorable character in each play. He also wrote realistic dialogue with a poetic eye, and his best dialogue touches eloquence. To illustrate, here are two speeches from the ending of *Thomas Muskerry*:

THE OLD PAUPER: A bright day, and the clay on their faces. That's what I saw. And we used to be coming from Mass and going to the coursing match. The hare flying and the dogs stretching after her up the hill. Fine dogs and fine men. I saw them all.[11]

And then after Muskerry's death, the pauper says:

And is he gone home, too! And the bees humming and all! He was the best of them. Each of his brothers could lift up their plough and carry it to the other side of the field. Four of them could clear a fair. But their fields were small and poor, and so they scattered.[12]

Although it may be tenuous, I see here a probably totally unconscious reminiscence of Antony's final speech over the fallen Brutus. But certainly it is in no way tenuous to see here a superb example of poetic realism.

V

In his indispensable 1929 volume, *The Irish Drama,* Andrew E. Malone wrote:

The name of Seumas O'Kelly is practically unknown outside Ireland, and even in Ireland his work has never had a large or widespread appreciation. His work has been most highly appreciated by discerning critics wherever he has been read, and his death at an early age in 1919 removed one of the most considerable, and most potentially valuable, of Irish dramatists. He contributed one great play and a couple of very good plays to the Irish Theatre, but it is as a novelist and a short-story writer that he is best known outside Ireland.[13]

In the 1970s, O'Kelly's short stories were re-issued, and Micheál Ó hAodha's dramatization of the masterly novella *The Weaver's Grave* has received some deserved attention outside of Ireland, but by and large O'Kelly's reputation is still an Irish one, and a semi-forgotten one at that.

Still, he must have been a remarkably sweet and charming person. Seumas O'Sullivan, for one, described him as the most good-natured person he had ever met:

> His was, indeed, one of those very rare natures which have the faculty of spreading a sense of well-being, of security, good-fellowship, healing, by their very presence. Bitterness seemed to fade out in the presence of Seumas O'Kelly, and quarrelling was impossible when he was in the company.[14]

O'Kelly was born in Galway and began his writing career as a provincial journalist. Moving to Dublin, he soon made a name for himself as an editor. He came under the influence of Arthur Griffith and so, when *The Playboy* riots occurred, he found himself for patriotic reasons out of sympathy with the Abbey group. Consequently, he gave his early plays to the Theatre of Ireland which made its greatest success with his best play, *The Shuiler's Child,* which had the often fine actress Maire Nic Shiubhlaigh in the main role. Several of his short plays were also staged by the Theatre of Ireland, but in November 1910, the Abbey produced *The Shuiler's Child* as a vehicle for Maire Nic Shiubhlaigh who had recently returned to the company. Subsequently the Abbey produced O'Kelly's *The Bribe, The Parnellite* and *Meadowsweet,* and with *The Shuiler* these plays seem O'Kelly's best.

The Shuiler's Child is a two-act, one-set, realistic play whose complicated plot is rather awkwardly compressed within this tight, short form. Necessarily, there are several coincidences, and much of the action is jumbled together in a smaller space than it would have plausibly been in life − a price O'Kelly and many other dramatists paid to fourth-wall realism. However, the play was intensely effective on the stage, partly because it concerns a mother giving up her child and an equally loving step-mother who is equally distraught at the possibility of losing him. This pathetic theme was as sure-fire in *East Lynne* as it is here, and it evokes an easy emotionalism that has often passed upon the stage for high drama. This basic fault is redeemed, transcended almost, by two remarkable virtues. First, there is the strong characterization of the two leading characters, the women who fight over the child. Moll Woods, the Shuiler, is a variation of the fallen woman with the heart of gold; that is, despite her hardness, she leaves the child and sacrifices her future to save his. Despite the *Stella Dallas* triteness and ultra-pathos, this business is well handled. Still, Nancy O'Hea, the stepmother, is the more convincing part; she is so loving and so protective toward the child that she becomes finely irascible, irritated by the social worker and a demon with her husband. But the first excellence of the play is the quality of the dialogue which is basically realistic but somewhat thicker than most realistic stage speech. The epigrams of the family friend are a case in point, and so also are the last moments of the play. There, O'Kelly rises to a couple of brilliant stage metaphors, and one of the speeches is reminiscent of the quality of Maurya's speech in the last moments of *Riders to the Sea*:

SHUILER [*Rising, calm, but wild looking*]: Ay, for the sake of the child. Everything is for the sake of the child. For the sake of the child they will be giving me gaol. The shirt I have is good enough now, Andy O'Hea. I will sing the streets of Galway again. . . Did you ever hear me singing in the streets? [*Standing close to him she sings in a voice hoarse with passion*]:

> His kiss is sweet,
> His word is kind,
> His love is rich to me —
> I could not in a palace find
> A truer heart than he.

That's the song I'll be singing on the streets of Galway. I'll have all the roads of Ireland before me, long roads and crooked roads. There it is before me, the narrow road with the grey stone walls on each side of it, stones that will look in the moon like the polished bones of dead men. And on the wide road, the broad wide road, I'll have before me the thick hedge on each side. There they are in May with the white blooms heavy upon the thorns. In the night they will stretch out in front of me, looking like two long arms holding up winding sheets to make shrouds for all the Shuilers of Ireland. . .[15]

I think that here O'Kelly, like Colum, rises to poetic eloquence. His metaphors have the directness of good dialogue and the preciseness and originality of poetry. In fact, the speech is so fine that it makes amends for much that is weak and usual in the play. It lifts the play.

The Bribe, produced by the Abbey on 18 November 1913, and *The Parnellite,* produced on 24 September 1917, are more quickly disposed of. *The Bribe* is a realistic play about nepotism, a workmanlike but not hugely remarkable thesis play. *The Parnellite* is a patriotic tragedy mirroring the effect of Parnell on the ordinary Irish community in the years from 1881 to 1890. It suggests, as does much of O'Kelly's work, that he wrote too much too quickly, and revised too little. The play fluctuates from straight-forward realism in Act One, to a satirically effective trial scene in Act Two, to an overly melodramatic welter of circumstances in Act Three.

What O'Kelly could accomplish at his best, however, is shown by the one-act comedy *Meadowsweet,* which was first produced on 7 October 1919, and most recently revived by the Abbey fifty years later in 1969. On it and on *The Shuiler's Child,* O'Kelly's dramatic reputation will, I think, rest. The play is a four-character one dealing, as do so many Irish plays, with the passion for land. The passions which spin the plot — land, social rivalry, economic marriage — appear in much fiercer plays, such as *The Building Fund, Thomas Muskerry,* Carroll's *Things That Are Caesar's* or Keane's *The Field;* but O'Kelly grafts them onto a typical comic reversal, the trickster tricked, that we might expect in Molière. And further the little play has an endearing quality that probably rises from the pervasive sprightliness of the realistic dialogue, a sprightliness which is a gay and tinkling counterpoint to the poker-faced action. The dialogue has some affinities with the best stage-Irish, for it is a bit heightened and more fanciful than the language of life. To judge by the photographically accurate dialogue of *The Bribe* and *The Parnellite,* and by the comic realism here, O'Kelly had a beautiful ear and knew exactly how to get what effects he wanted. The opening dialogue between Johnny Claffey and Maria Dempsey is reminiscent of the banter between Arrah and Shaun the Post in *Arrah na Pogue.* But, like Boucicault, O'Kelly avoids exaggeration and caricature, and the passage offers great opportunities for sprightliness and comic byplay:

JOHNNY: Are you at leisure?
MARIA [*Leaning out of window, angrily combing her hair*]: Leisure, how are you? Look at my hair!
JOHNNY: Is it only doing yourself up you are at this hour of the July day?
MARIA: My morning gone, striving to satisfy the appetites of Kevin Monahan's prize beasts. I might as well be throwing the feed over a half-door.
JOHNNY: Mind would you hurt your head. And it's a slave you are in this place. Give it up.
MARIA: And where am I to turn?
JOHNNY: Turn to the east.
MARIA: And browse on the wind?
JOHNNY: There you'll find myself, like the rising sun, I warming the world for you the long hours of the day.
MARIA: You're beginning already. . . . Off with you, Johnny Claffey.
JOHNNY: Listen, Maria.
MARIA: Worn out listening to you I am.
JOHNNY [*Rising*]: What prospects have you beyond myself!
MARIA: And a grand prospect surely is an ugly looking pike of a red-haired man. . .

JOHNNY. Maria, you're hard on me.
MARIA. Johnny, you're soft on me.
JOHNNY. Hard enough you may yet find it to get another as soft as what I am.
MARIA. There's no hurry on me. I have the whole country in front of me. The world is full of promise.
JOHNNY. A young Prince, I suppose, will come clattering up the road on a foaming charger, reeling with love over your dark beauty.[16]

If not consummately, this is fluently written and shows O'Kelly's charming talent for comic-realistic dialogue; and *Meadowsweet* must surely be ranked among the better one-act pieces of the Irish dramatic movement.

VI

Now, only about ten years after his death, St. John Ervine is fairly unread and unplayed, but he was a distinguished man of Irish letters who wrote accomplished novels, short stories, biographies, criticism and plays. He was an Ulsterman and, despite his strong ties with the theatre in Dublin, his Irish plays have never quite received their due in the South. His first produced play was *Mixed Marriage* which the Abbey did in 1911. It was followed by several one-acts, of which *The Magnanimous Lover* received nearly as bad and as stupid a press as did Synge's *Playboy*. In the Fall of 1915, Ervine was appointed manager of the Abbey and staged his finest Irish play, *John Ferguson*. This piece, with Dudley Digges in the beautiful role of Jimmie Caesar, was the financial salvation of what was probably America's most distinguished company, the Theater Guild. Although Lady Gregory disliked Ervine and wrote at length about his faults as Abbey manager, there is considerable evidence to suggest that Ervine was one of the better early managers. However, his tenure occurred during the First World War when the British were attempting to recruit in Ireland and when Irish nationalism was about to boil over into the Easter Rising. Ervine's British sympathies as well as his Ulster prickliness helped alienate him from many of the Abbey players, and on 29 May, 1916, they greeted patrons coming to the theatre with a handbill which read: 'To the Patrons of the Abbey Theatre. The Players regret having to disappoint their Public this week as they will NOT APPEAR at the Theatre under the present Manager, MR. ST. JOHN ERVINE. Full particulars will appear in the Press.' The company then dispersed, and in September a new manager was brought in.

After this Abbey stint, Ervine was inducted into the British army, and in the fighting lost a leg. After the war, he became drama critic for *The Observer,* and in 1928 and '29 spent a few months as a very sensible but sometimes abrasive guest critic on *The New York World.* His *John Ferguson,* as well as his *Jane Clegg* and *The First Mrs. Frazer* were highly successful in America. He wrote also a number of comedies for the British stage, somewhat in the style of Somerset Maugham. Still later he did some minor realistic plays with an Irish setting for the Abbey: the popular *Boyd's Shop* of 1936, *William John Mawhinney* of 1940, and *Friends and Relations* of 1941. Besides much journalism and fiction, he published highly opinionated biographies of Parnell, Craigavon, Wilde, Shaw and General William Booth.

However, here we are concerned with his early plays. His *Magnanimous Lover,* his first written if not first produced, is a one-act piece laid in a North-Irish village, and is an attack on piousity and the double-standard. Henry Hinde has seduced and deserted Maggie Cather, who has then borne his child as well as the scorn and ignominy heaped upon her by a provincial town. Years later, Henry having gotten religion, returns and offers to make her an honest woman. He is offering marriage purely out of religious self-righteousness rather than out of any feeling of love or even obligation. When Maggie sees that he will always regard her as a second-class human being, she refuses to have anything to do with him and sends him packing. The play is a little talky and over-long, and its points a bit belaboured; but it is a truthful, still-relevant attack at the kind of coldly ascetic religion which totally ignores humanity. Maggie Cather is a Nora Helmer *in petto,* as the play is a kind of diminutive *Doll's House.* The heroine of John B. Keane's *Many Young Men of Twenty,* set in a small Southern town of the 1960s, faced the same public contempt as did Ervine's Maggie fifty years previously.

Mixed Marriage, a full-length play set in Belfast in the first decade of the century, has a doubly descriptive title. First, the play tells of the marriage of a Protestant boy to a Catholic girl, despite the unyielding opposition of John Rainey, the boy's father. Second, it tells of another kind of mixed marriage, the union of Protestant workers with Catholic ones in a labour dispute. John Rainey, although a deeply engrained Protestant, is not a violent bigot, such as Ervine later drew in his one-act, *The Orangeman.* Rainey has sufficient tolerance and sense to be persuaded to use his influence in uniting

Catholic and Protestant workers. Still, this is only the beginning of tolerance, and all his past training and religious conditioning well up when he discovers that his son loves a Catholic girl. Then, feeling he has been tricked into tolerance, he goes out to break up the unified stand of Catholic and Protestant workers. And in the last act we see the consequences of his action: riots in the street and the accidental shooting of his son's wife. The beginnings of tolerance in the North are still only beginnings, and, as the various later imitations of this play suggest, *Mixed Marriage* is still pertinent.

Ervine based his story on the accidental shooting of a girl in some Belfast riots, but the play derives its strength from more than its real, inflammatory and highly dramatic situation. Indeed, what keeps the play from propaganda or melodrama is the realistic rightness of John Rainey. He is a taciturn, honest, basically kindly and well-meaning man who is not intelligent enough to shake off the doctrines of religion, even when those doctrines are pernicious. A religious principle, Ervine says, ceases to be religious when it is the antithesis of a human principle. Although the play is a realistic study of local manners, this general point and the craftsmanlike characterization lift it into universal significance. There are few plays in the South which have so honestly pitted the importance of man against the power of an entrenched institution. Two of the finest religious plays of the south, T. C. Murray's *Maurice Harte* and Gerard Healy's *Thy Dear Father,* seem to me to pull their punches. Probably the best such opposition is still in Seamus Byrne's *Design for a Headstone* and *Little City,* but Brian Friel in his recent *Living Quarters* and Thomas Murphy in *Sanctuary Lamp* have also made strong statements.

On 20 November, 1913, the Abbey presented Ervine's *The Critics,* a one-act *jeu d'esprit* which is in that excellent sub-genre of plays about plays, a group which includes such hilarious minor works as Buckingham's *The Rehearsal,* Fielding's *The Tragedy of Tragedies* and Sheridan's *The Critic.* In a note to the play, Ervine acknowledges his debt to Dublin dramatic critics for much of the dialogue. 'I lifted,' he wrote, 'many of the speeches, making no alteration in them, from the criticisms of "The Magnanimous Lover" which were printed in Dublin newspapers on the day after its first production.' The play, set in the foyer of the Abbey, is a *reductio ad absurdum* of the criticism of such plays as *The Magnanimous Lover,* Conal O'Riordan's *The Piper,* and of course Synge's *Playboy.* The story tells of the moral outrage of newspaper critics at a new play — one of the most outraged, however, not even having seen it. Ervine's point is the poverty of journalistic criticism, and his method is a realism so satiric that it simply quotes what was said. Perhaps some parts of life are really beyond satire.

The best way to commend the drollery of Ervine's satiric realism is to quote, and the play is so delightful that one may almost pick one's quotes at random. (The play being performed and criticised, incidentally, is *Hamlet.*)

MR. BAWLAWNEY: And then Yeats comes along, and he puts a fairy or a leprechaun in the play. Look at the piece to-night. The curtain was hardly up before a leprechaun comes on the stage.

MR. QUARTZ: I tell you it wasn't a leprechaun; it was a ghost.

MR. BAWLAWNEY: Well, it was a supernatural being, whatever it was. Yeats is always going after things like that. Look at his poems. . . .

MR. QUACKS: Poems, do you call them! Give me Moore's Melodies! . . .

MR. BARBARRY [*To Quartz*]: I never knew George Moore wrote poetry.

MR. QUARTZ: It's another Moore.

MR. BAWLAWNEY: And when Yeats and Robinson have finished the piece, Lady Gregory comes along and puts in some of her Kiltartan dialect. There was a speech to-night that I'll wager was written by her. Did you hear it, Quartz?

QUARTZ: I did not.

BAWLAWNEY: Yes, you did. It was the speech, 'That he is mad,'tis true: 'tis true, 'tis pity, and pity 'tis, 'tis true.' That came straight out of Kiltartan.[17]

Or, as Mr. Quacks later remarks: 'I can sympathise with the young man in the piece in his objection to the marriage, although I think his language was somewhat indelicate. Incestuous sheets! Sheets!! And women in the theatre, too. How can any nice-minded man sit beside a woman without feeling uncomfortable at the mention of these − these articles of domestic utility?' And this, of course, was a shaft at the alleged objection to the word 'shift' in Synge's *Playboy.*

Perhaps just one final quote:

MR. BARBARRY: . . . What do you call the chap that writ it?

MR. QUARTZ: A fellow called Shakespeare − William Shakespeare.

MR. BARBARRY: How do you spell it. . . That's not an Irish name, is it?

MR. QUARTZ: I never heard it before, but mebbe he comes from Belfast. They have queer names up there.

MR. BARBARRY: He does not, then. I come from Belfast myself, an' I never heard the name in my life. I tell you what! It's mebbe one of them Gaelic names. I wouldn't be a bit surprised now but he's a Gaelic Leaguer, I knew a man called Campbell writes his name in Gaelic, an' you can't tell how to say it. It's pronounced different from the way it's spelt. Mebbe, if you were to translate 'Shakespeare' into English, it means, 'Murphy'.[18]

The reference to Campbell is to Joseph Campbell, the Ulster poet, who spelled his name 'Seosamh MacCathmaoil.' At any rate, enough has been quoted to indicate that, using a perfectly flat and realistic diction, Ervine was able to get some remarkable satiric effects.

The best of Ervine's Irish plays, *John Ferguson,* was produced at the Abbey on 30 November 1915. In some ways it, as much as *Juno and the Paycock,* is the prototypical Irish play. By that, I do not mean that it is the best, but that in its theme and characters it is the most typical. It is about the most popular Irish themes of land, money and the arranged marriage. Like *Juno,* it is a family tragedy; that is, its larger social concerns are mirrored in the fortunes of a particular family. The family, as in *Juno,* is composed of mother, father, son and daughter. Although John Ferguson is no drunken loafer like Jackie Boyle, but a pious, elderly, sickly and admirable man, he is still as ineffectual as Boyle in holding the family together. The daughter, like Mary Boyle, has her sexual problems. She is not seduced, but is apparently raped by the villain of the piece, a grabber who has designs on Ferguson's farm. The son, like Johnny Boyle, is involved in violence and murder, and suffers from the nemesis of conscience. He secretly kills his sister's seducer and allows the blame at first to fall on James Caesar, the weak, self-pitying and contemptible grocer who is in love with the daughter, Hannah.

The play is a solidly structured, eminently convincing piece of realism that rises to moments of intense tension, but it has two or three weaknesses that keep it from being the masterpiece that it very nearly is. The great weakness is that the character of Caesar, who does not even appear in the final act, is so memorable, so fully three-dimensional, that he throws the play out of balance. He is a character like Falstaff, destructive to the intended theme of his play, but the best thing in it. And also one of the best things in Irish drama.

The character is also a fair indication of Ervine's fine realistic method. Although a character part, there is not one jot of exaggeration to Caesar, no theatrical heightening, no Joxerising. Ervine is perhaps the most clear-eyed realist among the early Irish dramatists; and it is a curious, but superb, flaw to have created a character so fine that he throws the play's structure out of balance and obscures the theme. Despite, or because of Falstaff, Shakespeare created a masterpiece. Ervine did not, and the reason is not the difference between prose and poetry, for the Falstaff scenes are in prose. The reason, of course, is mainly genius; but a contributory reason is the quality of Ervine's prose. It is a non-heightened, non-theatrical flat speech which differs from real speech only in being more selected and compressed; it is, in other words, what I have described as

prosaic realism. It differs from Colum's dialogue by never having
a remarkably apt word, a really happy or brilliantly just word, an
evocative word that vividly illuminates the ordinary words surrounding it. Talking of Boyle, I have admired such prose, and I admire
it in Ervine, but I would here like to suggest its limitations.

Jimmie Caesar is a brilliantly conceived character, but his language
is not. It is appropriate, functional, and in the theatre engrossing
enough. But it is never of the high eloquence of masterpieces. For
instance, here is Jimmie at an especially tense moment in Act Three:

JIMMIE CAESAR [*In a misery of self-abasement*] : But I'm not saved from
   sin, John. I didn't leave Witherow alone because I didn't want to kill
   him. I did want to kill him. I left him alone because I was afeard to touch
   him. My mind's the same now as it was when I went out of this house
   last night with murder in my heart. I want Witherow to be dead. I'd be
   glad this minute if some one came in the door there and told me he was
   dead. But I'd be afeard to lay a finger on him myself. That's the
   cowardliest thing of all, to want to commit a sin and not have the courage
   to do it. Do you think God'll be gratified when he thinks I didn't kill
   Witherow because I was too big a collie to do it?[19]

This is honest and penetrating, but it is not the language of great
drama. Jimmie Caesar and the high Art of the Drama demand more,
and that perhaps is why *John Ferguson* is not quite a masterpiece,
and perhaps also why Realism — despite all of its potentialities —
does not have the highest potential.

VII

Despite that last disclaimer, this essay is meant to celebrate
Realism, and I conclude with the dismal certainty that I have not
said enough. For instance, among the early realists, I have given no
example of the various and consummately craftsmanlike work of
Lennox Robinson, who probably at his best wrote smoother and
subtler dialogue than any Irishman of his time. I have given no example of T. C. Murray whose *Autumn Fire* rivalled, if not indeed
surpassed, Eugene O'Neill's *Desire Under the Elms*. I have given
no example from Rutherford Mayne's superbly comic *The Drone*.
Or no examples from — however, critics when they try to be ex-
haustive are usually only exhausting; and at best they should only
be signposts to the reader's own voyages of discovery. Yet perhaps
enough has been said to indicate that there is more merit in the realists
of the early Irish drama than the one adjective or the three sentences
they are usually allotted in books — oh! — too depressingly like
this one.

O'CASEY, THE STYLE AND THE ARTIST

A large part of the life of Clifford Odets' plays comes from his good remembering of what people do say in the Bronx. One hears that he sat in bars taking notes, and, for *The Flowering Peach,* resorted to the tape recorder itself. Sean O'Casey's dialogue, at its best, seems to me a little more 'creative' — i.e., created. He seems not just to remember and edit but also to develop the material, working it up to giddier heights of fantasy on his own.

Eric Bentley, The Life of the Drama

The style of O'Casey's plays has evoked two quite disparate reactions. Critics such as T. R. Henn, Raymond Williams, Ronald Peacock and Moody Prior, who are more concerned with drama as literature than as theatre, disparage it. As, for instance, Prior says, 'On occasion, O'Casey introduces speeches in a prose more elaborate and mannered than that which serves for most of the dialogue in the play, and the effect is almost invariably one of sentimental effusiveness which seems to encourage the poetic cliché.'[1] On the other hand, critics such as John Gassner, George Jean Nathan, Brooks Atkinson and Maxwell Anderson, who are more aware of the drama as theatre, admire O'Casey's style rather extravagantly. For instance, 'He has used language as though he were writing not for our modern picture-frame stage, but for the Elizabethan platform on which most of our great English drama was created' — to quote Gassner.[2]

Everyone seems to have a general impression of heavy rhythm, thick alliteration and dictional flamboyance, but so far both attitudes have remained impressionistic, and O'Casey's style has been subjected to little searching critical analysis. Although it is impossible in a short compass to say much about it, I would like to hazard a couple of general observations, and then to suggest a few specific peculiarities of the late plays.

It is now a commonplace that O'Casey's general dramatic technique underwent some notable changes, and his work is usually divided into an early, a middle and a late period. His dramatic style, however, is somewhat deceptive, for it initially appears, with one or two exceptions such as Act II of *The Silver Tassie,* to be much of a piece. In his rambles around Dublin as a young man, O'Casey had a retentive ear and a ready notebook, and certainly many phrases in his early plays which sound raciest to a non-Irish audience were familiar to Dubliners. This repertorial characteristic is most apparent in the early Dublin plays, but it still appears in the late ones. Similarly, in the early plays one notes such prominent characteristics as the singing of songs, the reciting of poems and the weaving of snatches of poems into ordinary conversation, the making of correct and incorrect literary and historical allusions, the making of malapropisms such as Captain Boyle's famous 'state o' chassis', the use of tag lines such as Joxer's 'darlin' and Fluther's 'derogatory', the use of repetition and alliteration, and the tendency toward rhythmical speech. All of these characteristics were present from the beginning, and all were sieved through a simple phonetic reproduction of Dublin speech.

However, the plays of the early period seem chiefly characterized by what might be called a heightened realism. The conjunction of the characteristics mentioned above produces an effect which is recognizably realistic, but nevertheless considerably richer than the speech of life. Little or nothing in the early plays could not have been said by a Dubliner; but, while an ordinary realist such as T. C. Murray, Lennox Robinson or George Shiels tried to reproduce the ordinary flavour of real speech, O'Casey tried to select the raciest of real speech.[3]

The dominant dramatic technique of O'Casey's middle period is — to tack the usual label on it — expressionistic. Years ago Denis Johnston noted hints of Expressionism in the basically realistic early plays, and O'Casey himself was fond of pointing to the allegorical one-act of 1923, *Kathleen Listens In,* as evidence that he had from the outset of his career been intrigued by the technique. The second act of *The Silver Tassie,* then, was only a seemingly abrupt leap into expressionistic statement; and so it was not really unpredictable that the entirety of the next play, *Within the Gates,* should be expressionistic. With *The Star Turns Red,* O'Casey began a partial retreat from Expressionism, and that play, although basically phrased in generalizations, has many realistic touches. In *Red Roses for Me,* the third act contains elements of Expressionism which lift a basically realistic mode into a momentarily lyrical one. After *Red Roses,* Expressionism does not entirely disappear from O'Casey's dramatic technique, but it is reduced to a contributory role.

The dominant rhetorical mode of O'Casey's middle period is that of dramatic poetry, and it was probably his misunderstanding of the nature of dramatic poetry that largely contributed to the eclipse of his reputation until the middle 1950s. By the canons of either heightened realism or lyrical poetry, much of the language of these middle plays is florid and overblown, and I myself a number of years ago attacked this style as blowzy and banal. I think now that such a view rests upon an imperfect understanding of the practical

function in a theatre of dramatic poetry. The techniques of effective dramatic poetry have eluded good poets from Browning and
Tennyson to Eliot and Auden, and it is far outside the scope of my
competence to discuss them. Very generally, though, it might be said
that the language of dramatic poetry works much like the language
of song. The words of a ballad or, for that matter, the libretto of
an opera may be insipid, but their alliance with a fine melody can
work a miraculous transformation. The 1969 revival of *The Silver
Tassie* by the Royal Shakespeare Company was not in all respects
successful, but the staging of Act II faithfully recreated O'Casey's
intention and thoroughly vindicated his language.

Certain characteristics of this middle style — particularly its highly
coloured and romantic diction — recur in the style of the late plays.
These late plays — especially *Purple Dust, Cock-a-Doodle Dandy,
The Bishop's Bonfire* and *The Drums of Father Ned* — are, I think,
versions of pastoral; and their style is a complex mixture of the
elements of O'Casey's early style, plus the addition of a few new
devices. Although the late plays belong to the same general genre,
they differ radically in tone, and so the overall style has in different
plays different emphases. Certain rhetorical techniques are stressed
in one play and appear much less significantly in another. This
rhetorical emphasis gives much of the particular individuality to each
play, and I should now like to illustrate what these devices are and
where they mainly appear.

I

Purple Dust is an extravagant farce in which everything is exaggerated. The Irish are overwhelmingly Irish — vastly quaint, pic-
turesquely shiftless, subtly cunning and fulsomely lyrical. The English
are immoderately English, the cows are super cows, the hens are
'entherprisin'' and lay their eggs with 'pride an' animation', the cocks
are so 'prime an' startlin'' that they scatter hens 'over hill an' dale,
lyin' on their backs with their legs in the air, givin' their last gasp,'
and even the lawn-roller is such a behemoth that one roll is
sufficient for the season ('An', faith. . . for every season after too.')
The lawn-roller in the Berliner Ensemble production looked big
enough to level the Parthenon.

The language of the play is similarly extravagant, and its notable
devices are parody, pastiche and mis-allusion. The most obvious
parody is an extravagant stage-Irish dialogue when the Irish are
guying the visitors. To take one instance from many, there is

O'Killigain's reply to Avril's 'Top o' the mornin', boys!':

Same to you, miss an' many of them, each of them fairer an' finer than the finest of all that ever brought the soft light o' the dawn at the peep o' day into your openin' eyes.

Similarly, when the English attempt to put on the Irish dialect what comes out is bald parody, half stage-Irish and half memory of Synge. Poges says, for instance:

Looka that, now. Arra, whisht, an' amn't I told it's strange stories you do be tellin' of the noble things done by your fathers in their days, and in the old time before them.[4]

There is also parody of the language of philosophical discourse, as when Basil says:

If we take the primrose, however, into our synthetical consideration, as a whole, or, *a priori,* as a part, with the rest of the whole of natural objects or phenomena, then there is, or may be, or can be a possibility of thinking of the flower as of above the status, or substance, or quality of a fragment; and, consequently, correlating it with the whole, so that, to a rational thinker, or logical mind, the simple primrose is, or may become, what we may venture to call a universal.

There is parody of the language of art criticism, as when Poges says:

Aaah! Precious, precious! The chaste form, the tender planes, the refined colouring, the exquisite design, the *tout ensemble* — they go into the un-discoverable deeps of the heart!

There is parody of the language of stock patriotism, as when Poges says of the English:

But every right-minded man the world over knows, or ought to know, that wherever we have gone, progress, civilization, truth, justice, honour, humanity, righteousness, and peace have followed at our heels. In the Press, in the Parliament, in the pulpit, or on the battlefield, no lie has ever been uttered by us, no false claim made, no right of man infringed, no law of God ignored, no human law, national or international, broken.

Several times there seems to be a pastiche of the language of Synge. The curtain line of Act One is a case in point. The Yellow-Bearded

Man peeps down through his hole in the ceiling and learns that Avril is 'careerin' all over the counthry on horseback with only her skin as a coverin'!' He then cries in aggravated anguish, 'Oh, isn't it like me to be up here outa sight o' th' world, an' great things happenin'!'

Often O'Killigain and the Second Workman will use Irish dialect not satirically but eloquently. At the risk of redundance, it might be called a heightened eloquence because it uses the conventional devices of moving dialogue that are to be found in Synge, Hyde, Lady Gregory, Fitzmaurice and M. J. Molloy, but uses them in a contrived profusion which probably should not, but usually does work. For instance, at one point the Second Workman remarks:

That was in the days o' Finn Mac Coole, before his hair was scarred with a hint o' grey; the mighty Finn, I'm sayin', who stood as still as a stone in the' heart of a hill to hear the cry of a curlew over th' cliffs o' Erris, the song of the blackbird, the cry o' the hounds hotfoot afther a boundin' deer, the steady wail o' the waves tumblin' in on a lonely shore; the mighty Finn who'd surrendher an emperor's pomp for a place with the bards, and the gold o' the King o' Greece for a night asleep by the sthream of Assaroe!

The third prominent rhetorical device is the erroneous allusion. Poges' conversation is full of them:

Especially the wild flowers that Shakespeare loved − the − the − er − er the primrose, for instance; you know − the primrose by the river's brim, a yellow primrose was to him, but it was nothing more; though we all actually know all there is to be known about the little primrose.

. . . the, the glory that was Rome and the grandeur that was Greece − Shakespeare knew what he was talking about when he said that.

Obviously these are in the play as comic illustrations of Poges' pretensions, but many are so drolly unexpected in their details that the play is lifted into the realms of lyrical nonsense. Just one last example:

POGES: Oh, if the misguided people would only go back to the veneration of the old Celtic gods, what a stir we'd have here! to the delightful, if legendary, loveliness of − er − er − er − what's his name, what's her name, what's their name? I have so often said it, so often in my mind, the chief or one of the chief gods of the ancient Celts?
SOUHAUN: Was it Gog or Magog, dear!
POGES [*with fierce scorn*]: No, no, no, no; try to think a little, if you really want to assist me. Can't you remember that Gog and Magog were two Philistinian giants killed by David, or Jonathan, or Joshua, or Joab, or Samson, or someone? It's the old Celtic god I have in mind, the one − what was his name?

SOUHAUN: Gulliver?
POGES: Oh, no; not Gulliver!
SOUHAUN: Well, I don't know the hell who it was.
POGES [*clapping his thigh exultantly*]: Brobdingnag! That was the fellow.

III

Cock-a-Doodle Dandy is usually considered among the best —
indeed, perhaps the best — of the late plays. Curiously, though the
play is not rhetorically too interesting. There is some humour in
Sailor Mahan's nautical diction, but this is a stereotyped device of
comic rhetoric and handled with no great flair by O'Casey. There
is a good deal of alliteration; in the first four or five lines of dialogue,
for instance, there is 'edge of evil . . . long an' leering . . . sinisther
signs . . . evil evocations . . . dismayin' decorations . . . lurin' legs.'
Some alliterative phrases, like 'mangled into a monstrosity' or 'th'
moody misery of th' brown bog', have a fine visual whimsicality;
many others, like 'constant consternation' or 'causin' constherna-
tion,' are not notably engaging. In only one or two instances does
O'Casey pull out the stops and gain a strong comic effect by the
device, as in:

Are you goin' to pit our palthry penances an' haltin' hummin' o' hymns
against th' piercin' pipin' of th' rosary be Bing Bang Crosby an' other great
film stars, who side-stepped from published greatness for a holy minute or
two to send a blessed blast over th' wireless, callin' all Catholics to
perpetuatin' prayer!

Perhaps the most engaging device is the 'Latin-lusthrous' language.
This would include the playful dog-Latin which O'Casey used also
in the autobiographies as a device of genial satire ('Oh, dana eirebus,
heniba at galli scatterum in Multus parvum avic, ashorum!'), the
Latinic saint's name ('St Custodius, pathron of th' police, protect
us!'),[5] and the incongruous misuse of polysyllables derived from
the Latin, and juxtaposed against the ordinary monosyllabic diction
of colloquial discourse. This last device is the most effective of the
three, and there are frequent instances of it. For example:

. . . so that you could controvert yourself into a dapper disturbance
. . . liquidate whatever it is with your Latin.
. . . th' circumnambulatory nature of a woman's form often has a detonatin'
effect on a man's idle thoughts.

Be on your guard against any unfamiliar motion or peculiar conspicuosity
   or quasimodical addendum, perceivable in any familiar thing or creature
   common to your general recognisances.
Aw, th' oul' fool, pipin' a gale into every breeze that blows! I don't believe
   there was ever anything engenderogically evil in that cock. . .
Looka, if you were only versed in th' endurin' promulgacity of th' gospels.

This comic device seems to work by 'fillin' broody minds with loose
scholasticality'.

Another effective rhetorical device is the personified adjective.
Here, O'Casey takes an inanimate noun, often a concept or a
generalization, and 'galvanizes' it into 'visuality' by a most animate
attached adjective. Some notable examples are:

> stern commotion
> jubilant store [of banknotes]
> lyin' hallucinations
> dapper disturbance
> rosy rottenness of sin
> reverberatin' fright
> bewildhered land
> half-naked finality
> rowdy livery
> taunting comfort
> somersaultin' prayers

He depends often upon a very visual verb choice. It might, in fact,
be called a poetic choice, for the best instances are apt and
unexpected:

. . . you could shutther th' world away with a kiss!
. . . she went sliddherin' down to hell!
. . . edgin' into revolt. . .
I'm not goin' to squandher meself conthrollin' live land-fowl!
. . . to perjure their perfection. . .
. . . I'd cyclonise you with a box [in the eye]!
If you want to embalm yourself in money. . .
. . . jet out your bitther blessin'. . .
You'll dhribble th' blackness of sin no longer over our virtuous bordhers!

III

The most noticeable rhetorical technique in *The Bishop's Bonfire*
might be called the derogatory epithet. Usually it is simply a

pejorative noun preceded by the word you. It is sometimes, but not always, modified by one or more adjectives or by an adjectival phrase. In the first act, the following appear:

> you holy hoodlum
> you rarefied bummer
> you spoilers of men's hopes and men's fancies
> you curses on Ballyoonagh
> you slimy touch of hell
> you buttoned-up delusion
> you dirty, evil-minded lugworm
> you huckster of hollow an' spiteful holiness
> you get
> you God's remorse for men
> you canting cod
> you blob of dung
> you muted jays
> you prayin' gaum
> you prayer-gasper
> you monkey-souled jays
> you bunch of destituted owls
> you menacer
> you neon light of ignorance and ruin

Only once or twice does O'Casey vary this form to something like, 'You're a nice Christian cut-throat' or 'Who are you to talk?. . . A dirty leaf torn out of a book'.

Had O'Casey used a less heightened diction, he would have written something like 'you crazy old fool', and this conventional and inexpressive criticism is the only other use of the form in the act. In a play like *The Drums of Father Ned,* where O'Casey is concentrating almost overwhelmingly on the device of allusion, the few derogatory epithets are, in fact, conventional. For instance, the only ones in Act III of that play are:

> you rascals
> you fool
> you dangerous fool
> you damned fool
> you bastards
> you hussy

And in *Behind the Green Curtains,* where O'Casey is still relying upon allusion for most of his effects, there are again few derogatory epithets. In Scene II, for instance, the only notable ones are 'you gabby slug', 'you painted doll', 'you festhered lily', and 'you ignorant, impudent little arcadian tart'. All of these occur on one page, and all but one occur in the same speech.

IV

O'Casey's use of allusion is governed by the necessities of dramatic dialogue. The prime necessity is that it be immediately apprehensible. If an audience must mull over the meaning or the implications of any particular line, then it cannot attend to what the actors are presently saying. This necessity does not absolutely imply that a dramatic author's allusions must be so obvious that any boob can understand them; but, when O'Casey weaves recondite allusions into his dialogue, he avoids obscurity by making his line function also on a non-allusive level. That is, a line of dialogue containing an obscure allusion will usually be perfectly clear and appropriate as literal statement to a person who does not recognize its reference.

Of the late plays, *The Drums of Father Ned* and *Behind the Green Curtains* are the most allusive, and *The Bishop's Bonfire* is the least. Act III of *Father Ned* can well illustrate the type and range of the allusions. First, among the conventional references to or quotations from something notable in the general history or literature of the world are the following:

Tom has a line, 'An' bid th' world farewell!' This seems to reflect a phrase from Thomas Campbell's 'Pleasures of Hope':

> Hope, for a season, bade the world farewell,
> And Freedom shrieked — as Kosciusko fell!

Later, Michael tries to remember the following lines from Tennyson's 'Locksley Hall', and Nora then quotes them:

> Many a night I saw the Pleiads, rising through the mellow shade,
> Glitter like a swarm of fire-flies tangled in a silver braid.

In the middle of the act there is a longish debate about religion, in which Lutheranism is referred to by the mention of Wittenberg, Calvinism by the mention of Knox, and Roman Catholicism by the mention of St. Robert Bellermine and Maynooth seminary. Shortly after there are mentioned 'the Anglican Thirty-nine Articles, the Westminster Confession. . . the Creed from the Council of

Thrent'.[6] This then is shortly followed by one of the most comic uses of allusion in the act:

McGILLIGAN . . . It'll all settled already! St. Pether, an' afther him St. Pathrick,   is our man, th' Rock on which our Church stands. What's yours piled   up on? On a disgraceful, indecent attachment of a despicable English king for a loose woman!
SKERIGHAN [*trying to overthrow McGilligan*]. Lussen, mon, lussen tae me!
McGILLIGAN [*furiously*]. I've lussened to you long enough − Henry the Eighth I am an' his harlot! Th' two saints of your church − Henry the Eighth an' a harlot! Oh, it makes me laugh − ha ha ha ha!

Michael then enters the conversation by referring to Joyce's 'a shout in th' street', and in his next speech refers to Bunker Hill, the French Revolution and the Soviet Revolution.

When Father Fillifogue enters, he cries, 'Are we goin' to be out in th' dear, dead days beyond recall? Me an' me boys of the old brigade'. The first line recalls the first line of G. Clifton Bingham's popular 'Love's Old Sweet Song', and the second line recalls Frederic Edward Weatherly's poem 'The Old Brigade'.

Then, Skerighan remarks, 'Wull ye no' tak' th' tumber awa' frae th' wharf tull th' muckle Lammas moon is glintin' on ye!' There may be a reminiscence here of Burns's poem 'The Rigs O' Barley', of which the first four lines are:

> It was upon a Lammas night,
> When corn rigs are bonnie,
> Beneath the moon's unclouded light
> I held awa to Annie.

The resemblance is not particularly close, but Burns was one of O'Casey's favourite poets, and O'Casey fairly frequently quoted from him.

Nora paraphrases a famous line from T. S. Eliot's 'The Hollow Men', when she says, 'Here's the whole town, currying a question to be answered, not with a whimper, but with a bang'.

There may be in Nora's comment, 'Doonavale has become th' town of th' shut mouth', a reminiscence of Brinsley MacNamara's novel, *The Valley of the Squinting Windows*. Undoubtedly, Murray's line, 'Dee trumpets blow, dee banners wave', reflects the first line of the second stanza of Burns's 'My Bonny Mary', which reads, 'The trumpets sound, the banners fly'. This is the poem, incidentally, from which O'Casey also took his title of *The Silver Tassie*.

Or, there is the following exchange:

BINNINGTON [*feebly*]. Bring me me bow of burnished gold!
McGILLIGAN [*attempting to be bolder*]. Bring me me arras of desire!

This is a slightly phoneticised version of two well-known lines from
the Preface to Blake's *Milton*. Blakes's complete stanza reads:

> Bring me my Bow of burning gold:
> Bring me my Arrows of desire:
> Bring me my Spear: O clouds unfold!
> Bring me my Chariot of fire!

O'Casey's use of Blake is broadly ironic, and he gains an effectively
ludicrous contrast by having these spirited lines emerge from such
feeble speakers.

O'Casey's most appropriate and deftest use of allusion is his frequent quotation of once-popular patriotic Irish ballads and poems.
He relies almost invariably on pieces which were once in the popular
consciousness, and few of his Irish allusions will be found in conventional literary anthologies, such as *The Oxford Book of Irish
Verse*. Instead, one will find his references in old, popular collections such as *The Spirit of the Nation* or *The Emerald Isle Song
Book*. O'Casey's Irish quotations, as well as his simple Irish allusions, function as a running subliminal reminder of the best of Irish
character and national aspirations. The Irish allusions are also made
in an interesting variety of tones. Sometimes the tone is a straightforward melancholy or regret, sometimes it is genially satiric, and
sometimes it is bitterly ironic. Practically always, however, the
allusions are used to criticize the shortcomings of modern Ireland
by the ideals of its past.

Act III of *Father Ned,* for instance, opens with a half-comic and
half-plaintive discussion of Irish mythology, in which reference is
made to Conn of the Hundred Fights, Brian Boru, Saint Columcille
and Young Angus. There may also be an allusion to Boucicault's
Sean the Post, in the reference to Jack the Cantherer, Doonavale's
postman. Or there is a comic discussion about Yeats and Oliver
Gogarty, and one of the lines — 'th' poet Yeats an' Gogarty were
goin' down Sackville Sthreet' — is a close resemblance to the title
of Gogarty's most memorable book.

A less recognizable allusion appears when Mrs. McGilligan tries
to make peace with the irascible Ulsterman Skerighan by quoting:

> So let th' Orange Lily be
> Thy badge, my patriot brother.

Mrs. Binnington then adds:

> Th' everlastin' green for me.

And Binnington and McGilligan chime in together with:

> An' we for one another.

The nobility of the sentiments, the broad and rather banal simplicity of the phrasing, the declamatory stiltedness of the delivery, and the complacency of the speakers all combine to produce an effect of mildly charming absurdity. However, the knowledge that the poem was not composed for the occasion by O'Casey, but was originally quite seriously intended and well known, insinuates a running truth of the play: although the Binningtons and McGilligans are amiably engaging, what they stand for is genially but firmly criticized throughout the play. This particular verse is from a poem called 'Orange and Green' or, more usually, 'Song for 12th July, 1843'. It was written by John D. Fraser, or Frazer, 'the poet of the workshop', who was one of the more popular writers for the organ of the Young Ireland movement, *The Nation*. The four lines which O'Casey uses are the conclusion of the first and final stanzas of Fraser's best-known poem.[7]

A few pages later, Father Fillifogue tries to stir Binnington and McGilligan to action in a speech which ends with the clause, 'youse'll be outlaws in a land forlorn'. O'Casey is here closely paraphrasing the first line of the chorus of Dr. George Sigerson's ballad 'The Mountains of Pomeroy'. Sigerson is not much remembered now, but he was for years the respected president of the Irish Literary Society in Dublin. His early translations from the Irish were pioneering work, and his 1897 volume, *The Bards of the Gael and Gall,* was influential and was known by O'Casey as a young man. Sigerson's stanza reads:

> An outlawed man in a land forlorn,
> He scorned to turn and fly,
> But kept the cause of freedom safe
> Up on the mountain high.[8]

A bit further on, Father Fillifogue ineffectually murmurs, 'I'll lead youse. Minsthrel boys, minsthrel boys, harps an' swords, swords

an' harps'. Here the humour is obvious because of the inevitable
memory of Tom Moore's still well-known and stirring song 'The
Minstrel-Boy', which begins:

> The Minstrel-boy to the war is gone,
>   In the ranks of death you'll find him;
> His father's sword he has girded on,
>   And his wild harp slung behind him.
>
> 'Land of Song!' said the warrior-bard,
>   'Though all the world betrays thee,
> *One* sword, at least, thy rights shall guard,
>   *One* faithful harp shall praise thee!'

Shortly after, a similar incongruous contrast is made between the
allusion to an heroic poem and an ineffectual effort in the play, when
McGilligan remarks lamely, 'Firm each foot, erect each head, an'
step together'. Father Fillifogue picks up the allusion by his desultory
reply, 'Like the deer on mountain heather'. Both men are quoting
fairly closely from the rousing opening stanza of M. J. Barry's poem
'Step Together', which originally appeared in *The Nation*. Barry's
first stanza reads:

> Step together — boldly tread,
> Firm each foot, erect each head,
> Fixed in front be every glance —
> Forward, at the word 'advance' —
> Serried files that foes may dread;
> Like the deer on mountain heather.
>   Tread light,
>   Left, right —
> Steady, boys, and step together![9]

Behind the Green Curtains is a more caustically critical play than
the genial *Father Ned,* and so the Irish allusions usually function
as mordant comments on the faults of the present. In Scene I,
Beoman functions as O'Casey's mouthpiece, and many of his comments are angry criticisms of the present, phrased in quotations from
Irish songs and poems. He scornfully criticizes a drolly ignorant version of heaven by calling it 'a Phil th' Fluther's Ball!' 'Phil the
Fluter's Ball' is, of course, a still popular comic song by Percy
French.[10] Or, when the Catholic artists are dithering about whether
to attend the funeral of a Protestant artist (which is actually an
allusion to the funeral of Lennox Robinson), and worrying about

whether their attendance will mean excommunication, Beoman lilts
softly a verse from the well-known ballad 'The Ould Orange Flute':

> So th' old flute was doomed, and its fate was pathetic,
> 'Twas fasten'd an' burn'd at the stake as heretic.
> While th' flames roar'd round it, they heard a strange noise;
> 'Twas the old flute still whistlin' 'Th' Protestant Boys!'

The song is followed by a satiric discussion of how the leadership
of Yeats is sadly needed now, and that is followed by Chatastray's
exhortation, 'For God's sake let us go in together'. To this, Beoman
replies mockingly from Barry's 'Step Together', which was also
used in *Father Ned,* 'Like th' deer on mountain heather'.

When Reena urges the artists to enter the church, Beoman makes
one of his few non-ironic quotations during the scene, and cries out
enthusiastically, 'Thou art not conquered yet, dear land'. He is
quoting from the first line of an anonymous poem called 'Thou Art
Not Conquered Yet'. Its first stanza goes:

> Thou art not conquered yet, dear land,
>   Though pale thy once bright cheek,
> Although thy lips of golden song
>   Now mournfully do speak.
>
> Although thine eyes have dimmed their hue,
>   And with cold tears are wet,
> Mother, thy heart beats proudly still;
>   Thou art not conquered yet.[11]

(Incidentally, the name 'Reena' may be an allusion to Ria Mooney,
who was the first 'Rosie Redmond', who was the first director of
Red Roses for Me, and who acted at Lennox Robinson's funeral
just as Reena does in O'Casey's play.)

Beoman is not the only character to make allusions. When it
appears momentarily that the artists have decided to enter the
church, Chatastray cries, 'Ah, sure, I never doubted you, said
Rory of the hill'. He is paraphrasing Charles J. Kickham's poem
'Rory of the Hill', and there is certainly some irony arising from the
contrast of the heroic attitude of Rory in the poem and the
cowardly one of the poets in the play. The poem in part
reads:

Right Hearty was the Welcome
That greeted him, I ween,
For years gone by he fully proved
How well he loved the Green;

And there was one amongst them
Who grasped him by the hand —
One who through all that weary time
Roamed on a foreign strand;

He brought them news from gallant friends
That made their heart-strings thrill —
'My soul! I never doubted them!'
Said Rory of the Hill.

V

John Gassner has written in a vague but sympathetic essay that
O'Casey's characters are often found to be 'lilting'. Probably he
meant simply that lilting was the highly coloured mixture of rhetorical
devices and vague rhythms. However, one narrower use of the term
'lilting' is song or snatches of song or even allusions to song.
Although other devices may be prominent in one play, and more
or less insignificant in another, I cannot think of an O'Casey play
from the earliest to the latest in which this lilting is not a significant
device.

As with allusions, the effect of song is various. Sometimes the song
functions simply as background music to raise the emotional
temperature. Often the songs suggest drolly or bitterly ironic attitudes, and often they are romantic or melancholy or stirring. Many
of them are Irish ballads, and these, like the allusions, are almost
always a reminder of some Irish ideal which is now withering away.

The effect of song can be tremendous in a play, and the effect
can hardly be judged by the words and notes on a page. But perhaps
generally we can say that the effect permeates the plays with a
buoyant lyricism. The characters in O'Casey's plays are always tilting
toward song, even at incongruous moments. For instance, there is
a speech in Act III of *Father Ned,* in which Michael uses song as
the clincher to an argument:

It might be a shout for freedom, like th' shout of men on Bunker Hill;
shout of th' people for bread in th' streets, as in th' French Revolution;
or for th' world's ownership by the people, as in the Soviet Revolution;
or it might just be a drunken man, unsteadily meandhering his way home,

shouting out Verdi's [*he lilts the words*] 'Oh, Le-on-or-a.'

VI

George Orwell, reviewing one of O'Casey's autobiographies, commented that the style was 'a sort of basic Joyce.' He undoubtedly meant that O'Casey's style was a simplified, and probably simple-minded pastiche of complexity. As any successful play must evoke a mass public response, rather than the individual private response asked by poetry or fiction, any complexity in its writing must have at least the appearance of simplicity. Indeed, on one level a play must still have more than the appearance; it must have the actuality of simplicity. The style of O'Casey's plays does, of course, work on a simple, primary level of overt meaning, but it is a good deal more than a pastiche of complexity. It is complex.

O'CASEY, THE STYLE AND THE MAN

Lately some critically minded people have questioned the authenticity of Sean O'Casey's autobiographies, but even the well-disposed have always admitted the absence of hard fact in those six remarkable books. Yet in the only essential sense, those books are as hard, exact and authentic as is possible for an autobiography to be. They catch, vividly and precisely and fully, the rich character of the man: and that, surely is mainly what a life story must do. If a life story, whether biography or autobiography, fails in that, it fails in everything.

Think of those many, fat, leather-bound, top-edges-gilt, two-decker lives of Great Victorians – books stuffed with facts and dates and everything possible except liveliness and life. Recently I read Sir Alfred Lyall's biography of Lord Dufferin, and learned everything important about the public man and practically nothing about the private individual.

The great life story in the English language is, of course, Boswell's *Life of Johnson,* which was published in 1791. In the nearly 200 years since then, Boswell has been contradicted and corrected, amended and amplified, and really superseded in every possible way except the intrinsic excellence of his portrait. If you want to know Samuel Johnson as a – in every sense – breath-taking man, you must not go to Walter Jackson Bate, but to Boswell. Similarly, if you want to know the breath-taking O'Casey, you must go to O'Casey.

Yet how can that be said when there is hardly a date mentioned in his entire six volumes? When, as some writers have plausibly argued, O'Casey ignored, suppressed, exaggerated and distorted? When central, even shattering facts of his life are not even touched upon? When his views of certain well-known public personages are so strange that those figures are nearly unrecognisable? When, for much of the later volumes, you get no exact or concrete sense of the ordinary, prosaic world about him? When, finally, his whole life story seems so camouflaged by, so utterly swaddled in, that famous and flamboyant prose style?

But perhaps the answer lies just there. In that. In his prose style. Buffon said that the style is the man. If an autobiography is honest and true, it reflects what the author saw that was to him important. An autobiography is made up of an arrangement of words, of a choice of words in certain chosen juxapositions. It is made up of a style, and a true and honest style is a reflection of an author's inner eyes as well as his outer ones. That is, of what he saw, but also of what he thought and felt about what he saw. That is, of his world, but also his brain and his soul. The true style is the true man, and nowhere more revealingly than when the man wrote about himself.

When O'Casey was alive, what he was like was known, casually or intimately, and more or less truly, by the few hundred people who lived with him, or worked with him, or talked with him. If you asked any of those people what he was like, their answers might have comprised a number of things — what he did, what he said, what he looked like, the expressions on his mobile face, how his voice sounded, his gestures, his habits, what kind of food he liked to eat, what kind of pipe tobacco he liked to smoke, certainly how he dressed, and maybe even how he would peer at the television with his face almost touching it. Yet most of those details would have been finally so trivial. When he was an old man, he looked marvellous — bony, frail, tolerantly cocky, bemused and with a costume too heroic for his weakening body although appropriate enough for his ever-strengthening spirit.

Now that he is dead, he can be a bit recaptured by his wandering shadow on a few feet of film and by the ghost of his voice on a few recordings. But to find more than the shadow of the funman, you have to go to what he wrote, and for a writer that is always the best and truest place to go.

I would say, then, that the truth and even the falsity of the man O'Casey is most fully and clearly to be found in what he wrote about himself. In the prose of the autobiography, the style was, and the style is, the man.

And whoever says O'Casey was lying in those six books knows nothing about autobiography or truth or style or men.

I

One could say that there are three kinds of prose writer — the individualist, the conformist and the zombie. All zombies write badly. Their medium minds have been programmed by the media, or starched by the literary protocol of the civil service, or embalmed by the jargon of methodologies that have to be methodical because they lack any better quality. The prose of zombies is laundered sludge, and sounds like 'Yours of the 7th inst. to hand.'

The prose of conformists comprises, in any language, much of

what is excellent and most of what is useful. It is the language of
a good, practical cook book; it is the language of a good, practising
journalist like Daniel Defoe; and it is the language of the greatest
satirist in English, Jonathan Swift. In modern English prose, Graham
Greene is a conformist, and so is Angus Wilson, and so is Frank
O'Connor.

The prose of individualists comprises a tiny proportion of what
is written in any language, and probably for the reason that individualists comprise a tiny proportion of the people in any country. An individualist's prose can be outré or ignorant or boring or
goofy or vulgarly replusive; but it can also be racy, thrilling, pro-
vocatively experimental and delightfully fresh. See the prose,
sometimes, of D. H. Lawrence; see the prose, sometimes, of James
Joyce; see the prose, often, of Dylan Thomas or E. E. Cummings.
See a good deal of the prose of Sean O'Casey.

O'Casey's style is so sufficiently individual that it invites parody,
as the prose of a fine conformist writer like Joyce Cary or Alan Paton
or Edmund Wilson does not. However, if you look into any collection of parodies, you will find there the great literary individualists
— Wordsworth, Whitman, Henry James, William Faulkner. What
is dangerous, of course, in individualistic prose is excess, even un-
noticed self-parody; and that probably is the price such a writer pays
for his eloquence. For every noble paean, such as Whitman's on Lin-
coln, there is paired the ludicrous spectacle of Whitman admiring
the smell of his armpits.

Of O'Casey's style, then, it must be said that it possesses liveliness
and vividness abundantly, wit fairly often, and eloquence sometimes.
It must also be said that it contains bad jokes and bad puns, that
it can exude monotony and sluggishness, and that it can emphasize
querulousness and bad temper. In sum, that the man can slip into
the manner, and the manner into the mannerism.

A simpler and, at his best, an ironic stylist like Hemingway could
develop from the simple tightness of *The Sun Also Rises,* to the loose
simplicities of *The Green Hills of Africa,* and into the elementary
floridness of *For Whom the Bell Tolls* or *Across the River and Into
the Trees,* and yet still be writing in basically the same style. Similarly,
O'Casey could modulate from the eloquent opening pages of *I Knock
at the Door* to the aridly jovial hectoring of much of his last essay,
'The Bald Primaqueera,' and yet still be writing in pretty much the
same style.

It was a style that did not so much develop as congeal. This
hardening from manner to mannerism paralleled the increasing
formulising of the dialogue of his plays, and partly derived

from his rigidifying character. A man's character does not change violently with age, but its more dramatic characteristics appear in bolder relief, and the bolder dramatic characteristics of O'Casey's prose got ever bolder as he himself got older.

There are probably three main characteristics of style, any style — the quality of the sentence structure, the nature of the diction, and the choice of rhetorical devices. Of these three characteristics, I would guess that a controlled sentence structure is both the source of greatest strength and the sternest brake against dictional or rhetorical excess.

The mature prose of O'Casey probably first appeared in his disgruntled and irascible collection of theatrical criticism, *The Flying Wasp*. In that book, his vehemently phrased judgments of successful playwrights of the day, particularly Noel Coward, or of influential but foppish critics, particularly James Agate, are not so much wrong as they are excessive. His barrages hit their targets, but blitzkriegs are scarcely necessary to squash pismires. The only necessity for the vehemence was personal. The airy and witless trivialities of Coward held the stage; the wit and intended profundities of O'Casey did not. Indeed, Coward was produced by C. B. Cochran who had produced *The Silver Tassie,* but who had turned down *Within the Gates* while retaining his long association with Coward. James Agate had liked Coward and criticised O'Casey. So the angry resentment of the better man for the more successful one erupted from many pages of *The Flying Wasp* and caused O'Casey's publisher to advise him not to bring the book out. Yet he persisted, and Macmillan did bring it out, and — Nathan aside — it is about the liveliest, funniest dramatic criticism to appear in English since Shaw's.

Still, *The Flying Wasp* is not a superb book, mainly because the author's spleen is too pervasive and too apparent. Its frequent excellence comes not so much from the author's feelings and opinions and certainly not from his embattled repetitions. It comes from a prose that is often so able, so controlled, and so wittily individual that the author's spleen is sometimes submerged and sometimes, in the sheer delight of writing, even abandoned.

See, for instance, the fable that takes up most of the chapter 'Sainte-Beuve, Patron of Poor Playwriters, Pray for Us!' The fable is too long to quote here, but it begins:

The Little Playwriters lived in the City of Dewymondroit. They were fed on dewberry dust and doughnuts specially made for them by the tribe of Criticonians who acted as the guardians in the daytime, and as their nurses at night. The Little Playwriters lived in dainty houses made of spun-glass, and where the sun shone these spun-glass houses were radiant with many colours so that each little playwriter looked like a little lizard encased deep in a diamond.[1]

Here the creative distance necessary to write a pastiche in the style of a fable becomes such fun for the author, that fun wins out over spleen. Or, to take another example from the same book, consider the excellent effect of sentence structure and concluding alliteration in these remarks about Coward's play, *Design for Living*:

. . . as if life would end because Gilda slept with Leo instead of Otto, and passing through a period of four years, all the arguments, all the explaining away of the sun and moon and life and death, have been the screaming of Otto because Gilda went to bed with Leo, the screaming of Leo because Gilda went to bed with Otto, and the screaming of Ernest because Gilda decides to leave him, and return to her orbital movements from Leo to Otto and from Otto to Leo till the final curtain puts a veil over these poor wincing worms in a winecup.[2]

Yet, fun as it often was, *The Flying Wasp* was of but minor importance; and the prose that was its glory required a bigger scope than criticism, a deeper tone than hectoring, and, most especially, a more humane theme.

II

That scope, that tone and that theme, O'Casey found in the story of his life; and in it he wrote his most witty, vivid and eloquent prose.

The very opening sentence of volume one, *I Knock at the Door,* was evidence enough that here was prose stretched to a task both nobler and more demanding than any the author had ever attempted before. That opening sentence is about three pages long, stretches over eight paragraphs, and contains eight or nine hundred words. It is masterly.

Its structure emphasises a powerful simplicity of statement and emotion, laid over a complexity of form that is tense, tight and architectured. The form is so complex and so long that paragraphing is made to do duty as punctuation, and actually the paragraph break becomes a kind of super semi-colon. Yet the mortar of punctuation is never enough to hold a badly wrought sentence together. You can splash around commas and dashes galore, but, if you have written a mishmash of syntactically illogical clauses in awkwardly arbitrary lengths, no punctuation is potent enough to work. You cannot glue mush.

O'Casey's sentence is a consummate exploitation of the parallelism of words, phrases and clauses, and the exploitation of periods stretched and stretched but never broken, and the exploitation of balances held and reversed and repeated and still tenaciously held.

The sentence is too long to quote here, but its first paragraph introduces a woman in childbirth, and then quickly expands into a detailed panorama of the bustling late-Victorian city of Dublin, and then expands even more broadly into an evocation of the bustling, late-Victorian world view. And then finally the passage contracts again in two more longish sentences to a view of the woman in childbirth, now superimposed on both previous montages. The passage, then, has the fluid and economic swiftness of a good film. This is how it concludes:

And the woman in child-pain clenched her teeth, dug her knees home into the bed, became a tense living mass of agony and effort, sweated and panted, pressed and groaned, and pressed and pressed till a man child dropped from her womb down into the world; down into a world that was filled up with the needs, ambitions, desires, and ignorances of others, to be shoved aside, pressed back, beaten down by privileges carrying god-warrants of superiority because they had dropped down into the world a couple of hours earlier. The privileges were angry and irritable; but the round-bellied, waggle-headed, lanky-legged newborn latecomer kicked against the ambitions, needs, and desires of the others, cleared a patch of room for itself from the trampling feet and snapping hands around it; was washed, napkined, and fed; added on three, four, or five ounces of weight every week, taking most of it from his mother and a little from the life around it; and so grew gradually, and gathered to itself the power, the ignorance, the desire, and the ambition of man.[3]

To me, writing such a passage is like moral calisthenics or aesthetic prayer. The necessity of creating, through a complicated sentence structure, a unique, appropriate and effective form can hobble the excess of spirits, temper the rhetorical exuberance, and, if this does not sound too silly, even make the writer momentarily a better man. Conforming to form, whether philosophical or ecclesiastical or aesthetic or rhetorical, can subordinate an individual's faults and quirks to the race's excelllence.

However, even in this accomplished first passage of *I Knock at the Door,* there is a discernible overtone of O'Casey's most disturbing faults. Reading *The Flying Wasp,* one would have said that its author appeared as generally vital and vivid, but as frequently veer-

ing back and forth from the joyous to the disgruntled. These basic
qualities also set the tone of the great biography. In its best passages,
such as the opening, the discipline of sentence structure engaged the
author in the problem of creating an effective but complicated form
and, therefore, imparted a control and contained his excess feeling.
In that first passage, dissatisfaction appears but does not overwhelm;
it is held, restrained, as a contributing part of the overall structure.
Similarly, his vitality is restrained from exploding into mere bump-
tiousness, and his vividness held from descending into a pointless
parade of gaudy devices.

With less restraint from structure, one of his major characteristics
can take the centre of the stage. Then his legitimate critical dissatisfaction can turn into an unedifying querulousness that hurts much of
the autobiography in its later pages. Or it can turn into a vitality
that finally becomes enervating because it is so long-winded and its
content so repetitious.

The first volume of the autobiography appeared in 1939 and the
last in 1954. In those years, there was some modification of the style,
and diction and devices of rhetoric finally became more important
than sentence structure. Perhaps O'Casey was influenced by the plays
he was writing at the time. Modern plays generally have few long
speeches, and so there is less opportunity to do much that is complex or powerful with the sentence structure. In the later plays, the
most notable characteristics of the language are diction and the use
of certain rhetorical devices. In the prose of the later autobiographies
and essays, diction and rhetorical devices seem also the paramount
characteristics.

In the first passage of *I Knock at the Door,* there is a considerable
range of diction. O'Casey goes from the colloquial 'mucking about'
to a literary phrase like *'tour de force.'* His references range from
the universally recognised 'Hollywood' to the moderately obscure
'Aesculapius.' His style ranges from the naiveté of a Beatrix Potter
to a touch of Elizabethan rhodomontade. But everything is held in
a tension never overstrained and never incongruous. The content is
fused into a form by a tight control of the sentence structure.

When the structural restraint is relaxed, it is not only the author's
personal characteristics, but also his use of diction and rhetorical
devices that puts matters askew. O'Casey's chaste diction can flower
into floridness, and his favourite rhetorical devices can wax into mere
vices. Here, for instance, is the ending of the late essay, 'The Bald
Primaqueera':

Today I heard on the wireless of a fifteen-year-old lass diving into the

sea to save a boy of ten. The boy was saved, she was lost. And of a
policewoman who risked her life on a roof-ridge to save a baby which a
half-mad father had in his arms, ready to jump off the roof, baby and all,
had the brave woman not snatched it from the frantic father. Brave woman,
brave teenager lass. Ah, to hell with the loutish lust of Primaqueera. There
are still many red threads of courage, many golden threads of nobility woven
into the tingling fibres of our common humanity. No one passes through
life scatheless. The world has many sour noises, the body is an open target
for many invisible enemies, all hurtful, some venomous, like the accursed
virus which can bite deeply into flesh and mind. It is full of disappoint-
ments, and too many of us have to suffer the loss of a beloved child, a wound
that aches bitterly till our time here ends. Yet, even so, each of us, one time
or another, can ride a white horse, can have rings on our fingers and bells
on our toes, and, if we keep our senses open to the scents, sounds, and sights
all around us, we shall have music wherever we go.[4]

This passage starts off simply and clearly, then veers into an ill-
considered and rather garbled sentence, followed by a couple of
fragments that are utterly O'Caseyan and utterly bad: 'Brave woman,
brave teenager lass. Ah, to hell with the loutish lust of Primaqueera.'
And then followed by a sentence whose diction stamps it as inimitably
O'Casey's: 'There are still many red threads of courage, many golden
threads of nobility woven into the tingling fibres of our common
humanity.' But by this time the red and gold have faded because
they have been pressed into service so often, and the fibres are not
taut enough to tingle. However, the rest of the passage picks itself
up, even despite the sad personal aside that does not belong, and
concludes with a moving and memorable sentence.

In his later prose and plays, O'Casey writes too indulgently. His
control wavers, and he tries to bludgeon through on personality,
splattering alliteration and semi-puns about in a fine fury of ferocious
frenzy, a merry mélange of mingled-mangled metaphor, and a
gorgeous galimaufry of glittering gaudiness. One wades through that
stuff, knowing that he was too much an artist to be very bad for
very long. But even his most tarnished tinsel is thoroughly his, and
the faults of his individualistic prose seem often more revealing than
the qualities of his conventional contemporaries.

He was often simple-minded, or had a chip on his shoulder or
a score to settle, but he never wrote to hide or to cheat. More often
than not, he amused us with a brilliantly creative whimsy, and he
moved us with a marvellously felt eloquence.

The style certainly was the man, and what a man!

THE INFLUENCE OF O'CASEY

Influence moves three ways — backwards, forwards and sideways. There are the figures and forces that influenced the writer; there are the figures and forces that the writer influenced; and there is much inconsequential critical nattering about the whole business — from which stricture, naturally, the present essay is not excluded.

How to handle influence has always been amorphous. Usually it has been enough for the critic to discern influence, and we then assume that all has been said. Perhaps the reason is that influence seems the one solid fact among a multitude of conflicting opinions and cloudy theories.

For critics, the idea of influence has usually meant that a writer has read, has admired or loathed, and has been moved to restate or refute attitudes, or to parody or to pastiche techniques. Just how often does that really happen in a major writer? In Tolstoy, in Dostoevsky, in Proust, in Faulkner? Not much, I should think. Yet it remains convenient for critics to pontificate that O'Casey's, or anybody's, literary influences were such and such, and thus and so. And there the matter usually rests, in a pleasant and genteel fuzziness, in the theory at the end of the *cul de sac*.

All of this, of course, is a prologue to imply that the premises of this essay are somewhat dubious.

I

However, it is conventional to say that O'Casey's major literary influences were the ebullience of Elizabethan rhetoric, the eloquence of the King James Bible, the diction and opinions of Shelley, the techniques and jolliness of Boucicault, and the rhetoric and opinions of Ruskin and Shaw. But what this comes down to is that O'Casey reminds us, in some analogous way, of such writers — in opinions, techniques or quirks of style. However, when some genius like Brooks Atkinson speaks of O'Casey's Elizabethan flamboyance (what Elizabethan? Bacon?), his *aperçu* quickly congeals into dogma, never investigated but inevitably cited. It is all very traditional and cosy, and the author, O'Casey or whoever, has now been given some literary credentials.

Actually, the matter of credentials was a problem with O'Casey.

Despite all of the recent chatter about how he was a member of the affluent middle-class, he became a poorly-paid manual labourer with not much formal schooling. So in looking for credentials, his early academic proselytizers were basically attempting to establish that he was worth talking about, and not merely a rough genius with a flair for transcribing slum dialogue. I have played that academic game myself about O'Casey. To make ignored merit intellectually respectable and, therefore, to put money in my man's purse, and to promote theatrical productions for him, it was good tactics to write him a set of impeccable literary credentials. How sound such a purely literary provenance was may have been a moot point. The one unmoot point is that the merit resides in the man's actual work and not amorphously in his presumed antecedents.

The overt literary influences that O'Casey assimilated were possibly to his detriment. For instance, what he got from Shelley was enthusiasm, excitement about writing, love of beauty and a penchant for extravagant rhetoric. These qualities are fine for a casual reader, but dangerous for a professional writer. In some of O'Casey's apprentice poems and pre-*Gunman* political polemics, these qualities appear at the worst. He realised in later life the floridness of this early writing, but he did not always recognise new versions of floridness in, say, *Within the Gates* or *Red Roses for Me*.

There were at least four facets to him as a writer — the lyric, the caustic, the playful and the sombre. When the lyric was wedded to one of the other three, it worked beautifully; and Donal Davoren, the Shelleyan poet who is regarded with a partly caustic eye, is a finely realised creation. When the lyric was not wedded to one of the other tempering moods, it worked less well; and the Shelleyan Ayamonn Breydon is regarded with a lyric admiration that makes him slightly less noble but much less convincing than Jesus. Unadulterated Shelley was adulterated Sean.

That unadulterated literary influence would explain, for instance, a character like Mary Boyle. Mary is the last of the New Women, and not the first of the liberated. Her older sisters are Nora Helmer, Vivie Warren and Nora Burke; and the only strange part of the business is that Mary was born a quarter of a century after her sisters.

Much of O'Casey's influence was sub-literary. Look at the loveable masterpiece, *Juno*. What is at the center of the plot but a will? And who is the central character but Tom Robertson's Old Eccles? And who is the ingenue but the girl who is seduced and abandoned? And what is the worst line of dialogue but, 'My God, Mary, have you fallen as low as that?' Archibald Carlisle couldn't have said it better. In other words, *Juno* is so good that it transcends the awfulness of its influences. What is good is what O'Casey himself brought to it.

But how about the previous literary treatment of Sean's most O'Caseyan subject matter, the Dublin slums? It has, I trust, by now become impossible to say that one of Sean's great attributes was that he discovered a rich new subject matter. In the drama alone, his old nemesis A. Patrick Wilson had been there first, followed by, among others, Daniel Corkery, Oliver Gogarty, Randal M. Lamb and M. M. Brennan. Of the six or seven noteworthy slum plays before the *Gunman,* O'Casey saw certainly only *Blight* by Gogarty and Joseph O'Connor. Yet all of the earlier slum plays, but one, bear a distinct family resemblance to *Juno;* and that one, Corkery's comedy *The Onus of Ownership,* has strong points of resemblance to *The Shadow of a Gunman.*

The resemblance of the best known of those plays, *Blight,* to *Juno* is basically that the Tully family is not awfully different from the Boyle family. The reason, however, is an almost generic necessity of choosing a slum family as the microcosm of what is wrong with the slums. Poverty, drunkenness, prostitution, disease and early death are the topics to be embodied in the unavoidable typical members of a slum family – that is, father, mother, son and daughter.

Hence, the general resemblances between Wilson's *Slough,* Gogarty's *Blight* and O'Casey's *Juno.* The differences, however, are major. *The Slough* and *Blight* address themselves to a number of specific social issues, while *Juno* makes one generalised statement about man's inhumanity to man. Also, the texture of *Juno* is just incomparably better – the dramaturgy, the characterisation, the quality of the writing. So really it would hardly matter if O'Casey had known all of this previous work; he handled the material so individually that the point of influence is just beside the point.

O'Casey became a highly aware and well-read man, and the size and scope of his library would seem admirable to all but the most pedantic of academics. Yet even later, as a sophisticated reader, his most literary influences seem to me his most pernicious. For instance, two of the most important stylistic ones were the incongruous pair of George Jean Nathan and James Joyce.

The Flying Wasp is a most Nathanish book, adopting many of Nathan's broad strategies and even some of his specific tactics. The rephrasal of Noel Coward jokes, for example, into their earlier music-hall and Joe Miller equivalents is straight from Nathan. The whole breezy insouciance, the immediacy as of a man speaking, and the irreverence are all also quite Nathanish. However, Nathan's most noticeable quality is his style, and some of his stylistic techniques are used, but not really assimilated by O'Casey. Much of Nathan's effect is based on the incongruous juxtaposition of words from different levels of language; and this technique, incidentally, was also the chief weapon in the rhetorical armoury of his colleague, H. L. Mencken. At its best, when the technique is coupled with a witty sense of contrast and a wide-ranging vocabulary, it provides a series of shocks. It unexpectedly and drolly topples over the class barriers of language. When well used, the technique is a reader's delight, but even at its most glittering it is hard to take in large doses. For Nathan and Mencken and even Wodehouse, this technique became the chief weapon in their rhetorical armoury. It grew finally to be as much a limitation of style as was the paradox for Chesterton.

O'Casey was never as hard-edged in his dictional juxtapositions as was Nathan, and so there is in *The Flying Wasp* less of wit and sophistication, but more of insouciance and − whenever the chip falls off O'Casey's shoulder − rather more of winning gaiety. There is, in fact, loss and gain. O'Casey is more fun and Nathan is more businesslike, but one never feels that Nathan is harbouring a deeply felt personal grudge. A hard-edged rhetoric is a fine bastion against the intrusion of personal feelings, as in Dr. Johnson's letter to Lord Chesterfield. There is a sour-grapacity in *The Flying Wasp* that probably also accounts for the attacks going on too long. A tougher rhetorical control knows when to stop.

Nathan's appeal to O'Casey was in part a delicious playfulness with words, and O'Casey's own delight in playing with words was notable as early as *The Shadow of a Gunman*. His playfulness was quite in the comic tradition of Dickens and Ben Jonson − that is, of the linguistic variations from a civilised norm made by comic types and stereotypes. The ignorant parody of legalese in Mr. Henderson's letter is exactly in the central tradition of English comic writing. O'Casey's great stylistic achievement, for purposes of comedy, was an Irish dialect better than his predecessors' − among whom were Shakespeare, Thomas Sheridan the Younger, Richard Brinsley Sheridan, Dion Boucicault, J. M. Synge and even Bernard Shaw. (His predecessors in fiction, from Maria Edgeworth to Somerville and Ross, had made a somewhat stronger showing.)

The example of Shaw was, of course, not lost on O'Casey, and Shaw had a broader mastery of rhetorical techniques than had Nathan. The glitter of a succession of single sibling phrases was Nathan's; the glow of an integrated mastery of rhetorical techniques was Shaw's. Shaw stood on more battlements than O'Casey, stood longer, and came away less scarred. O'Casey became more personally involved than Shaw in his fights; the reason was partly temperamental and, therefore, partly rhetorical. At his most engaged, O'Casey would throw in his personality and the handful of rhetorical devices that had come to express it. At his most intense, Shaw would throw in the personna of G. B. S., and remain detached enough still to command his amazing range of rhetorical techniques. (Not to diminish O'Casey's perception here, one should mention that he was almost alone in pointing out that Shaw was, among other things, a lyrical writer.) Their writing personalities were, however, different. Shaw was the Superman from whose chest the bullets bounced harmlessly, the Galahad whose armour was never pierced. O'Casey was more the Launcelot or Gawain or, much more, the noble and fatheaded Roland who made the final issue cluster around him, and who fell. In any event, O'Casey mastered the parts of rhetoric that appealed to his individuality; and so rhetorically he was not really a son of G. B. S.

The greatest rhetorical glitterer of O'Casey's time was James Joyce. Joyce mastered the range of rhetorical techniques as had Shaw, and then added some of his own, but Joyce used the content to show off the technique, and Shaw finally said that the man who has no content has no style. O'Casey was hugely attracted to some of the Joycean possibilities. In the late plays and in the autobiographies, where O'Casey was honing his style into its most Seanian apotheosis, the example of *Ulysses* and *Finnegans Wake* was much in evidence. George Orwell, reviewing one of the late autobiographies, called O'Casey's style a kind of basic Joyce. O'Casey — to cite an example of the worst kind of literary influence — and O'Caseyans have always regarded the phrase as an insult and an affront. Pushing aside the pejorative flavour of the phrase, though, one might not find it a bad description. O'Casey took from Joyce mainly the portmanteau word, the triple or quadruple level pun. At his best, he got from it a pervasive and breezy inimitability. The inimitability arose, I think, because O'Casey differs from Joyce in the levels of his punning. O'Casey simplifies punning, and so becomes at his worst glib without being funny; Joyce complicates punning, and so becomes at his worst turgid without being funny.

The conventional pun works in two different directions simultaneously. The Joycean portmanteau word has more than two directions of meaning, but some of the directions are only hints, shadows, suggestions or overtones of meanings rather than the pun's two or more exact but different statements. O'Caseyan wordplay tends to be a half-pun. It lacks sufficient underpunning; it has one exact meaning and one shadow of meaning or, even worse, one pointless meaning.

A non-O'Caseyan example would be the title of Diana Dors's autobiography, *Swingin' Dors,* which is clever in one direction and pointless in another. Many of O'Casey's word plays are also half-puns. He remarks that Cassidy goes hopping along, which has some pertinence for the character of Johnny Cassidy, but little for or from Clarence E. Mulford's cowboy. He remarks, 'A terrible beauty is Borneo'; the traditional ballad ending tacked onto 'born' entails a flip criticism, but the intrusion of the place is neither funny nor meaningful.

O'Casey developed in his late work a highly individual style, capable of great comic effect and, with discipline, of considerable lyrical possibilities. However, the best qualities of this style were his inventions and not his borrowings.

Perhaps the best kind of influence upon O'Casey was neither a literary attitude nor a rhetorical technique, but the germ of an idea. Let me give one example.

On March 17, 1925, there was produced at the Abbey Theatre a piece in six scenes entitled *Anti-Christ* by Frank J. Hugh O'Donnell. Frank O'Donnell was not Yeats's *bête-noir* who had attacked *The Countess Cathleen.* He was a Galway man who came to Dublin toward the end of this century's second decade, who wrote some literary journalism, a few poems, several plays which were produced in Dublin, and one which was produced (somewhat financed by him) at the Q Theatre in London. Later he became a successful shirt manufacturer in Dublin, and he died only recently. O'Casey was friendly with him and present at the first night of his play.

O'Donnell was not a very good playwright; and *Anti-Christ* was not an awfully good play. It tells of the aftermath of the Great War, of the remembered suffering of the participants, and of their bitter disillusionment with the post-war world. A blind veteran, John Boles, inaugurates a popular movement of war veterans to combat what is wrong with the brave new world. The movement grows until it becomes dangerous to those in power, and then Boles is arrested and sent to an asylum. Contemporary critics of the play thought that a chief weakness was that the story was told too unconventionally. Boles does not appear in the last scenes; other characters take over and tell us about his story. Actually, the plotting is rather interesting and has some thematic justification. The chief weakness of the play is that its politics remain utterly vague, and the audience never really knows what Boles is specifically for or against.

On the credit side, there are some interesting points. In two scenes, O'Donnell flirts with Expressionistic techniques, and thereby accomplishes some effective shortcuts in his fable and some broadening of his scope. Scene 2 has seven sandwichmen, carrying bills which read, 'Watch Out, Anti-Christ is Here.' They march onstage, line up their sandwichboards all the way across, and talk about the progress of Boles' movement. Scene 4 is similiar in intention and conveys information about the plot, but is a realistic vignette between a nameless newsboy and a nameless policeman.

The situation and attitude of *Anti-Christ* are those of *The Silver Tassie*. There is no Expressionistic scene of the War itself, but the chorus of maimed and wounded is quite like the O'Casey characters. In fact, the concluding scene of *Anti-Christ,* like the concluding scene of *The Tassie,* takes place at a dance, and contrasts the anguish of the veteran with the callousness of the present. Indeed, it may be instructive to quote the conclusion of O'Donnell as a contrast to the conclusion of *The Tassie.* John Drysdale has been a conscientious objector and violinist, who later won a V.C., but lost his arm. George and Joe and Alf were sandwichmen in Scene 2:

GEORGE. Oh here, John, chuck it. Maudie, Joe and Alf came up for a short hop and now you chime in and spoil the show.

JOHN [*Suddenly aware again*]. Oh aye. Dance around, dance to hell. Up in the Asylum John Boles can bawl and roar and shout himself deaf, but what do you care? What does anyone care? All hopping and flapdoodling. Tomorrow when people read the papers they'll just say to one another 'So Boles was mad, poor devil. It's well they got him in time.' Then they'll all go back to their ruts again, all falling mechanically into their grooves — the blind doddering idiots. And Boles can keep on shouting and braying — blind — blind — do you hear — for you and all of you. [*He is overcome again*].

GEORGE. It's his own look-out.

JOHN [*Staring at him*]. His own look-out! You don't give a damn. No, of course not — nor anybody else doesn't give a damn. It's none of their business. You'll just keep jazzing about — jazzing about. Oh, why should *you* care, or why should the others care. It's my arm that's gone west, it's the other fellows who died, it's Boles that's been put into the Asylum. Keep jazzing on our bones. It's our look-out.

MAUDIE. John, you are taking it too seriously.

JOHN [*Getting more calm*]. Thanks, Maud — yes, perhaps I am. Perhaps I'm a fool — and — maybe we're all mad. Yes — we're all mad. I'm taking life too seriously. I'm in the way here amongst the wise young generation. I'll go — and I won't forget, Maud, we're mad — all mad — [*He laughs hysterically as if he discovers some great truth. He goes to the door and hisses back at them.*]

Men died for you. You lot of fools, *mad men.* [*He screams with laughter and goes.*]

GEORGE [*When he is gone*]. John's absolutely out of control.

ALF. Anyhow I was too young to join up. And if those fellows did fight what the devil else could they do?

MAUDIE. Oh chuck it — chuck it. What's the use of worrying? Aren't we alive today and dead tomorrow?

JOE. For the love of Mike, Alf, hit the piano a wallop.

GEORGE [*Deliberately*]. If I hear anyone mention Boles, War or Anti-Christ anymore, I'll break his face. [*He puts up his fist in exposition.*]

MAUDIE (Offering her lips). Except me, George.

[*He looks at her and smilingly accepts the offer. Then 'If Winter Comes' electrifies the atmosphere once more, and Maudie is teaching again. 'La-la-di-daw-di-daw. Left-one-la-la-di-daw.'*][1]

The situation and, indeed, the whole play are so reminiscent of the *Tassie* that it seems certain that O'Donnell's piece was the germ of O'Casey's. In Scenes 1 and 3, O'Donnell rises to some fairly effective tirades, but generally there is no comparison between his conventional and awkward dialogue and O'Casey's irony and eloquence. There is here no question of one author plagiarising another, but there is an instructive instance of how influence worked best for O'Casey. He saw a play embodying ideas like his, a play not really fully worked out, with only the mildest and occasional satire and humour, with little individual emotion, but with a fine ironic situation at the end. No doubt what went through his mind was, 'I can do this infinitely better', and that was what he went and did. And the distance between O'Donnell's original and O'Casey's variation is a symptom of the critical length that perhaps the best influence needs to be seived through.

II

O'Casey had more impact than influence, and it seems impossible to say that here was an O'Caseyan school, or that there were the sons of Sean. It is hard to follow genius if one's resources are only talent. If one pastiches, one produces a pale carbon; if one parodies, one produces a grotesque exaggeration. Genius, after all, is exaggeration enough.

There are a few forgotten neo-Syngean pieces by Con O'Leary, Fergus O'Nolan and others; and there is little reason to disinter them, for the original Synge is so much better. What is imitable is talent; and so some of the early Cork writers — Murray, Robinson, Ray,

MacCarthy — seem in their serious work more similar to each other than any later writers seem to O'Casey.

O'Casey's language, like Synge's, was a weapon like Philoctetes' bow or Arthur's sword: no one else could wield or draw it. And, of course, that language developed ever more inimitably and unimitably. It could, and has been parodied, sometimes unconsciously even by O'Casey himself, but it has never really been awfully well emulated.

The O'Caseyan situation which seems to have been most imitated is the family situation in *Juno*. One could point to a play by Louis D'Alton, a play by Bryan MacMahon, a couple of Galway plays by Walter Macken, a Northern play by Joe Tomelty, a Belfast play by John Boyd, and to an almost brilliant Glasgow play by Paul Vincent Carroll. But again the reason may simply lie in the choice of a nuclear family as an obvious microcosm. Certainly Paul Carroll would have vehemently repudiated any suggestion of O'Casey's influence.

The famous O'Caseyan mingling of comedy and tragedy was something that he had no patent on. A dozen geniuses and several hundred hacks had done it before, and his great impact was simply that he did it so memorably that he shocked everybody. In his early plays, Walter Macken seemed trying for a Galwegian equivalent of *Juno's* comedy and tragedy, but wound up closer to farce and melodrama. It was only later when Macken went more his own way that he wrote his best.

The use of song and dance and spectacle? O'Casey used them so well that, when wedded to his dancing words, he seemed on the verge of opera or circus. But song and dance and spectacle were part of the drama from its beginnings, and a lively later writer like Brendan Behan used them in his own way and not in O'Casey's. And as for Patrick Galvin, James MacKenna or Jim Sheridan . . . well, I'll pass.

The use of irony? Sophocles, Shakespeare, Ibsen and H. J. Byron put that to some use, as did even Sean's *bête-noir* Alfred Hitchcock.

On those who came later, he had more impact than influence.

III

Perhaps it is ungracious to touch upon a third kind of literary influence — a kind, I think, that only occurs with writers as individual as O'Casey, i.e., their opinions, their mannerisms and their techniques descend to their commentators. The pleasure that one has in first discovering a fine writer like, say, Graham Greene or Joyce Cary or Alan Paton or J. G. Farrell, is different from the delight in discovering a writer so individual as O'Casey. With Cary, the pleasure glows; with O'Casey, it pulsates. My generation was cowed by a bombardment of remarks like, 'As Mr. Eliot remarked. . . .' And so the discovery of an O'Casey generated not only a terrific enthusiasm for his literary accomplishment, but also a violent fervour for his opinions. If one were a critic, one became then a missionary affirming life (in defiance, I suppose of something else . . . death, capitalism, middle age, God knows). And one also acquired a pronounced tendency to emulate the master's own prose style. For instance:

O'Casey is eminently, ultimately, foremost and sideways a man of the theatre, and I think that his flamboyantly theatrical last plays prove that point. *The Drums of Father Ned* insists that, although the Green Crow is aging, his caw is neither hoarse nor thin, but clear and piercing. With plays like *Purple Dust, Cock-a-Doodle Dandy,* and *The Drums of Father Ned* in his nest, the Green Crow can no longer be ignored by us nor rebuffed by his countrymen. Ignoring O'Casey now is only a measure of our own poverty, for it is too increasingly apparent that O'Casey, like W. B. Yeats and good Irish whiskey, improves with age.[2]

This effusion was mine, but it seems only pale lavender compared to the purpler neo-Seanian rhapsodies that have flowed forth since. All of that, however, was but enthusiastic emulation and harmless enough. What seems of some real harm to O'Casey criticism is its violence, arrogance, pomposity and bad manners.

In the late fifties or early sixties, Ronald Ayling, David Krause and, I suppose, I were constantly in armed and irascible combat against any benighted wretch who assaulted Sean's character or works. And although we were probably more often right than wrong (as there was a lot of stupidity rampant), we surely set an unfortunate pattern. It was a pattern that we were emulating from the Great Man himself, but it was the worst of his influence.

DENIS JOHNSTON'S HORSE LAUGH

Denis Johnston has usually spoken about his plays with a diffident ambivalence — even with a kind of defeated chagrin. When, for instance, *The Moon in the Yellow River* was revived Off-Broadway in 1961, Johnston pointed to an anecdote in the play, about how a man accidentally shoots the horse he is riding in the head, and remarked how different audiences had reacted differently to it:

> I have noticed with interest that in Dublin and in Paris this passage gets an immediate explosion of mirth. In London, after a moment of uncomfortable hesitation, there follows a strange delayed reaction that builds into a laugh lasting for almost half a minute, and which usually interferes with the following dialogue. On the other hand, when performed in the Polish or in the German tongues, I am informed that there is no response whatsoever. I am not certain what conclusions can be drawn from this data, but I am quite insistent that such a story — even among horse lovers — is a good example of what might be described as an authentic Irish joke, a fact that in itself may be one of the real things that is funny about the Irish.[1]

There is an engaging lack of swank and ego here, but I suspect that it disguises a hedging against failure or even against a stupid kind of success. In actuality, it is difficult to read Johnston's plays without perceiving that he knows precisely what he is doing and precisely how to get his effects. He has paid the most meticulous attention to the most minute detail. So if audiences, whether Irish or American or Polish, do not react appropriately, I should say that usually something is wrong with the production, occasionally something could be wrong with the audience but only rarely is something wrong with the dramaturgy.

Still, Johnston's plays do take some living with, both because of their general high quality and because of their diversity of styles. During his active career, critics found him an uncomfortable writer. He was hard to pigeonhole, for his work was sometimes complex in statement and usually unpredictable in technique. Only now, at the end of his career, is his work finally being intelligently assessed and assimilated.

I should imagine that the critical appraisal of Johnston will go on for some years. When, however, the pundits have had their say,

I would put my money on two of his plays, *The Moon in the Yellow River* and *The Scythe and the Sunset,* as finishing by a nose in a dead heat. His first and possibly best-known play, *The Old Lady Says 'No!',* will, I think, fade in the stretch. Johnston has never been properly credited for his originality in this play of adapting the allusive technique of Eliot and Joyce to the drama. However, many of his allusions elude Irish audiences; and in the recent adequate, but hardly inspired Abbey Theatre revival, even this strongpoint appeared weakish. The texture of the dialogue was thinner than one had supposed, and much of the bright young satiric 1920s banter now appeared more clever-clever than witty.

Johnston's own favourite play, *A Bride for the Unicorn,* could have had, with a little luck, the success of a Cocteau or, later, a Beckett play. However, at this late date, it does seem, if not the work of a clever-clever satirist à la *The Old Lady,* at least the work of a clever-clever intellectual. It would take an elaborate staging to do the piece well, and so it is probably as unrevivable as Colum's *Balloon,* O'Casey's *Within the Gates* or O'Neill's *The Great God Brown.*

Much else by Johnston seems highly revivable, and I am not sufficiently the prophetic punter to say which play could break out of the pack to place or to show in the homestretch. The trial play, *'Strange Occurrence on Ireland's Eye',* must probably be preferred over its original, *Blind Man's Buff,* and as a thoughtful courtroom melodrama must rank among the best of that usually brainless genre. The Swift play, *The Dreaming Dust,* has fine possibilities for actors and surpasses the half-dozen other Swift plays almost as much as *The Old Lady* surpasses the two dozen other Emmet plays. Still, the structure of the piece is overly schematic, and could — as I have remarked somewhere — illustrate not so much the Seven Deadly Sins as the seven deadly scenes. If *Strange Occurrence,* however, is a thoughtful courtroom melodrama, *The Golden Cuckoo* is that even rarer bird, a thoughtful farce.

I have been stressing how unique Johnston is, but it is the uniqueness of the consummate adaptor. His works are really adaptations of standard forms: the gloss on the medieval morality in *The Dreaming Dust,* on the patriotic melodrama in *The Old Lady,* on the broad farce in the *Cuckoo.* I mean this statement in no perjorative sense, for, as Eric Bentley has pointed out, most of Bernard Shaw's early plays made similar use of traditional forms and yet were utterly individual.

Johnston has distinctly disassociated himself from Shaw, whom he has called the 'Good Old Wenceslaus of Ayot St. Lawrence —

a monarch who was always a pleasure to read, a headache to listen to, and utter confusion to agree with.' Despite that disclaimer, Johnston's plays are full of Shavian reverberations; *The Golden Cuckoo* seems a variation of *Saint Joan,* and *The Moon* has its obligatory discussion scene.

Johnston is most Shavian in his mastery of the traditional tricks of the trade. Shaw's uniqueness had roots in the tried and true. The freewheeling and relatively ignored late plays (such as *In Good King Charles' Golden Days* or *Too True to Be Good* or *The Apple Cart),* as well as the middle masterpieces (such as *Heartbreak House* and *Saint Joan* and *Back to Methuselah),* all came out of the anti-melodrama of *The Devil's Disciple,* the anti-romance of *Arms and the Man,* and the anti-pantomime of *Androcles and the Lion,* the modern version of the chronicle play of *Caesar and Cleopatra,* and the neo-Ibsenism of *Widowers' Houses, The Philanderer* and *Mrs. Warren's Profession.* All of these early pieces derived a basic strength from variations of the forms and techniques of Shakespeare, Boucicault, Planché, Ibsen and a dozen other veteran practitioners of conventional stagecraft.

Johnston in this respect, then, is thoroughly Shavian, and any analysis of his technique must not begin with his own clever contributions to technique in *The Old Lady* or *The Bride* or *The Dreaming Dust,* but in his mastery of timeworn and traditional devices.

I

I propose to illustrate my point by *The Moon in the Yellow River* because it is one of Johnston's best and best-known plays, and because its conventional plotting, characterization, dialogue and spectacle surprisingly support a most unconventional theme. On the stage, the play has never been entirely successful, but it should have been. With conventional audiences and commentators, the play failed; with more urbane audiences and commentators, it achieved a limited success. With really perceptive audiences and commentators, it still, I think, might triumph. The recent English production of Granville Barker's *The Madras House* was something of a much belated vindication of that extraordinary masterpiece; *The Moon* deserves a similar production and a similar vindication.

Before considering how Johnston's dramaturgy should work, we might instructively glance at how it has worked upon its most notable audiences.

The Moon was first produced by the Abbey Theatre on 27 April

1931, and was apparently an attempt to write a play that would fit
the Abbey stock company. There was a Maureen Delany part, an
Eileen Crowe part, and a part that was inevitable for F. J. McCormick. Yet Johnston was not really an Abbey dramatist, particularly
in those heydays of George Shiels, Brinsley MacNamara and the great
comic eccentrics of O'Casey. Johnston was obviously Anglo-Irish,
nominally *avant garde,* and had made his local reputation with the
Gate — hardly the kind of person to endear himself to the lower-
middle class Abbey actors and the predominantly bourgeois Abbey
audience.

About this production, Johnston wrote:

It was gently sabotaged by most of its original Abbey cast who until 1938
played it with that subtle air of distaste with which experienced actors can
dissociate themselves from the sentiments expressed in their parts.[2] On its
first night it had one of those very mixed receptions that usually presage
a riot on the second. However, this never quite materialized, although I
waited in some apprehension in the green room for another of those sum-
monses to the stage that have nothing to do with a curtain call. All that
it got was a rough deal from the newspapers, which complained that its
humour was feeble, that it had no visible plot, and that it 'introduced some
coarse levity on the subject of childbirth'.[3]

The conventional reaction might be suggested by Joseph Holloway's
resumé:

'Thank God!' rang from Mr. Campbell all over the house when Arthur
Shields announced that the author wasn't in the house. It was the best line
of the evening, and it echoed the sentiment of most present who had been
thoroughly bored by an undramatic play that was a sneer from start to finish
of everything one holds dear in Ireland and of the Catholic faith. The last
act had a very uneasy passage, one felt it in the air, and had the author
had the courage to face the audience I am sure hisses would have been plen-
tiful. The play was talky, undramatic rubbish laden with untruths. What
it was all about was a puzzle to the world.[4]

On 28 February, 1932, the play opened in New York, produced by
the Theater Guild, with Claude Rains as apparently a superb Dobelle
and with Henry Hull as a very American Darrell Blake.[5] *The New
York Times* reported:

It was not, in many ways and for a number of reasons, a thoroughly satisfac-
tory evening, but it was one which stimulated the imagination — in itself
an unusual achievement for the current theatre — and provided

several fine and absorbing moments. 'Provocative' is the word which may
partially, if somewhat inadequately, cover the situation.

    The Moon in the Yellow River is certainly not a literal and explicit play.
It is beclouded with symbolic references which, on this side of the Atlantic,
are obscure to those not thoroughly acquainted with Irish Free State history
and politics. It rambles conversationally along a good deal of the time,
discussing poetically and philosophically a variety of topics. It lacks the
dramatic effectiveness of an O'Casey play, or the rich warm flavor of an
Irish folk piece. It follows autochthonous moments with moments of
vagueness and generalization and then breaks out in some rather explosive
melodrama. In short, by rule of thumb measurements, Denis Johnston has
not written a good play. But he has written one you are likely to remember
after many admittedly good plays have run their course.

    . . . Much of what he has to say is interesting, but some of it is not so
interesting in the theatre, where action still rules. 'This is not a country;
it is a debating society,' is, in substance, the remark of one of the characters.
That also holds true for Mr. Johnston's discursive play. . . .[6]

In his long Sunday review, the *New York Times*'s Brooks Atkinson, a generally sound critic somewhat given to gush, wrote:

    Unlike Li Po, who was drowned in the attempt, Denis Johnston has suc-
ceeded in embracing 'The Moon in the Yellow River.' He has imprisoned
the most vital part of Ireland, within the three acts of a bouncing drama.
Not being a literal play with a single, concrete story and a literal argument,
it deceives the expectations of ordinary theatre-going. Like *The Lower
Depths,* it is discursive on the surface. But it is sound and searching
underneath, and it is heavily freighted with the truth of character. No other
recent Irish play has contributed so much to an understanding of Ireland.
Mr. Johnston does not explain; he irradiates. [7]

Part of this description seems more appropriate for J. Hartley
Manners than Denis Johnston; however, Atkinson goes blithely but
confusingly along to suggest that the play has lots of story, but that
the story 'is only a fluttering incident in an ebullient drama. What
makes *The Moon* . . . such a vital play is its racy, full-blooded
characterizations. . . .' Then, after developing his point about
characterization, he concludes with a typically lyrical peroration:

When a native Irish playwright gives us a beautiful, poignant drama steeped
in the spirit of his own country it behooves the plodding theatregoer to pull
himself up by his bootstraps. For an understanding of contemporary Ireland,
The Moon . . . is better than Synge or Yeats and better than the urbanized
O'Casey, Mr Johnston has captured a vital part of Ireland.

In 1934, the play was produced at the Malvern Festival and then brought to London for a limited engagement. *The Times* remarked:

> Mr. Johnston's tragi-comedy . . . suffers from a surfeit of ideas. It is a rare fault in the theatre, and easy in this instance to condone, so supple and revealing is the dialogue, so unstrained and abundant the underlying comic inventiveness. Because the author's study of Irish playboyism carries him over too many tricky currents of thought — the conflicting ideals of the visionary Republic and the existing Free State, peasant resentment of industrial progress, philosophic Nihilism and its painful resolution — his play loses direction and ends on the shoals of sentiment; but the comic episodes are delightful, and the analysis of character is shrewd and diverting. . . . Altogether, a play of rare quality and excusable faults, which, even in its difficult ending, bears the impress of an original and engaging mind.[8]

With some cast changes, the play transferred to the Haymarket and went to a run of about two hundred performances. Again *The Times* remarked:

> It would have been a pity, indeed it would have been a reflection on the London theatre, if this play had vanished from sight at the end of its limited run. . . . it has the structural fault of ending twice — once when a power house, symbol of industrialism in the Irish Arcady, is accidentially wrecked . . . and again when a morose neurotic realizes that there lives again in his hated daughter the mother who died giving her birth; but these are by no means ruinous flaws upon a play of rare theatrical vitality. . . . But as it is presented the play — its structural faults forgotten — triumphs as a group of fantastic portraits, each with an intense theatrical vitality of its own, given life by imaginative and satiric dialogue which is as stimulating as it is amusing.[9]

The play was revived Off-Broadway in 1961, on which occasion Howard Taubman wrote in *The New York Times:*

> Mr. Johnston's story about Ireland in 1927 is not all of a piece, either in mood or toughness of fibre. But it is the stimulating work of a man with a rousing aptitude for the theatre and with a joyous relish of the wonderful diversity and crustiness of the human species. In a season tinged heavily with mediocrity it is heartening to encounter a literate playwright. . . .
> They are a pleasure, these Irish, as they blather, philosophize, bicker and bumble. There is only a trace of the stage comedian in them, for Mr. Johnston has seen them freshly. . . .
> *The Moon* . . . has lost something in immediacy in the thirty years since its appearance. But it is still saturated by the Irish gift for mocking and mourning the contradictions of Ireland.[10]

After being once rescued by an infusion of money from a backer, the production limped on for a total of forty-eight performances.

The play has had quite a few other productions, but these are probably the important ones, and their reviews interestingly run a gamut from curt dismissal to rapturous admiration. The plot has been thought clever, faulty and even non-existent. The characterization has been called realistic and been called theatrical. The theme has been seen as pro-Irish and anti-Irish, as trenchant and muddled. Obviously, either the playwright is hopelessly confusing, or his audiences are awfully confused. I should like to suggest that the fault is not primarily the playwright's.

II

Many commentators have been troubled by both the plot and the theme of *The Moon in the Yellow River*. Often, the plot has seemed a group of discursive conversations interrupted by explosions of melodrama or by eruptions of sentiment. Often, the theme has seemed more an anthology of the author's diverse pre-occupations than the coherent statement about a single topic that one finds in most plays. Johnston's theme, however, rises out of his plot, and in discussing the play it is difficult and unnecessary to divorce the two.

The plotting of Act I is both highly craftsmanlike and highly conventional. It broadly works like this: an outsider, Tausch, is introduced into an eccentric Irish household; and, as he is the voice of reason, common sense, industry and courtesy, we see initially through his eyes and we judge by his judgements. However, by the end of the act, the procession of fey Irish eccentrics has so engaged our sympathies that we have grown tolerant of their humourous naturalness and a little critical of Tausch's stiff correctness. The audience, in other words, has become inclined towards a tolerance of their lawless and anti-civilized but apparently harmless behaviour, and toward an intolerance of Tausch's lawful, civilized but possibly harmful behaviour.

Most of the act is concerned, as most first acts in any play, in introducing, identifying and describing these characters. And, at the end of the act, in the best Horatian, Jonsonian and Drydenian fashion, an entry is made into the actual action: that is, Blake announces his intention to blow up the powerhouse, and Tausch begins the counter-action by secretly phoning the police. Most of the intellectual content of Act I is not, nevertheless, the play's real theme. It is an introductory theme, and no more than the old

Shavian topic of the difference between the Irish and the rest of the world.

This contrast between civilization as embodied in Tausch and anarchy as embodied in the varieties of Irishmen is consistently made by jokes and witty juxtapositions, so that the bulk of the act is comic in effect. Even the most portentous action, the plan to destroy the powerhouse, is made by a comic, although not ridiculous, statement. All of this is quite Shavian; as in Shaw's early plays, comic actions and illustrative jokes emphasize an alternative truth to the conventional one that the audience entered the theatre with. As Shaw's Broadbent comes to seem to the audience the romantic rather than the practical man, so also are we made to see in Johnston's play a truer truth than the usual theatrical platitude. In making us tolerant of his charming, anarchical Irish, Johnston has pushed us to see the truth behind the paradox and the lie behind the platitude.

This theme of Irish anarchy versus world civilization may be seen, then, not as the false theme of a comic prologue, but as a conditioning to accept the real, if paradoxical, truths of the major theme which is developed in Act II. (Some years ago, during a production of *The Dreaming Dust,* Johnston told me that it was impossible to implant in an audience's mind something that it did not already believe. *The Moon* and, of course, practically all of Shaw are just such attempts, however; and Johnston's remark may possibly be taken not only as repudiation of Shaw but also of his own early work. As substantiation of this disillusionment with audiences, I might cite another remark that Johnston made at the same time. His main character in *The Dreaming Dust,* Jonathan Swift, at one point said in effect, well, I must go out and write *Gulliver's Travels* now. As this seemed an exceptionally bald line, I suggested that we cut it, but Johnston replied that it had to stay in because three-fourths of the audience would not know that Swift had written *Gulliver's Travels.*)

The centre of Act II is a Shavian discussion scene in which the characters sit down and give their votes and their reasons for blowing up the powerhouse. In *The Quintessence of Ibsenism,* Shaw wrote that the discussion was going to be the most vital part of the new drama. For once, Shaw seems to have been wrong, and the drama has continued to demand the naive simplicities of story-telling, and story-telling, and more story-telling.

Putting content into a play is like trying to contain water in a sieve. Johnston seems well aware of this fact and counterpoints his static discussion against a containing action. Tausch and the audience know that the police will arrive at a certain time, and so

Tausch attempts to prolong the discussion while making furtive glances at the prominently displayed clock. In other words, Johnston brilliantly has his cake and eats it. Having his cake means developing the tension of an engrossing action. As in Shaw, though, the argument is as engrossing as the plot; and that argument, in which Johnston finally opts for impracticality and idealism and the old ways, seems to me the central theme, if not the final point of the play.

(Curiously, in an introduction to *The Old Lady Says 'No!' and Other Plays,* Johnston remarks that in Dublin, *The Moon* 'has always been suspected of harbouring a superior ascendancy smile at the expense of the noble native, and it has never been popular there on that account.' And yet nothing could be closer to de Valera's ideal of an Arcadian rural Ireland than the backward look of the play's theme. The point is, no doubt, that a conventional patriotic statement must be made in a conventional, traditional way. *The Old Lady* says rather the same thing as *The Moon,* but says it backward, satirically rather than admiringly. If it has been somewhat more popular than *The Moon,* the reasons are undoubtedly Micheál Mac Liammóir's playing of Emmet and Dublin's penchant for snickering at any topic whatsoever. In any event, *The Old Lady's* popularity was relative; it was no *Juno;* it was not even *a Passing Day.*)

Having debated, if not yet quite decided the point, the playwright must conclude the action of the police arriving, and then he must introduce a new action for the third act. Dramaturgically, the new action must be introduced to conclude Act II and, even more important it must top the previous action. Conventional dramaturgy demands a big first act curtain and a bigger second act curtain. Many second act curtains are cliffhangers and leave the audience wondering what will happen next. Johnston's second act curtain is a cliff-faller and leaves the audience startled, nonplussed and wondering what has just happened. It is a dangerous device because it demands that the audience react unconventionally. In a note, Johnston says:

> Occasionally a curtain falls on the second act without as much as a clap of a hand from the audience. And, oddly enough, this phenomenon is regarded by those who know the play well, not as a disgrace, but as an indication of a really fine performance.[11]

And, one might add, such a reaction is the most experimental of writing because it demands an untheatrical response.

Part of Johnston's untheatrical daring has to do with when Blake is killed and how the audience regards Blake. In conventional dramaturgy, you can kill off the bad guy at the end of the play, and,

if you can pull off that *tour de force* called tragedy, you can also
kill off the good guy at the end of the play. Hotspur is enormously
appealing, but he has got to go for thematic reasons, and the
audience is satisfied enough about the matter because he is faultier
than the hero. (The ritual killing of Falstaff at the end of *Henry
IV, Part II* is not nearly so successful because Falstaff's faults have
become much more enchanting than Hal's virtues.) In Johnston's
play, Blake is killed too soon, only two-thirds of the way through,
for conventional dramaturgy; and also the audience has begun to
like him. Only the fact that Johnston has a stageful of other
appealing eccentrics to take up the slack palliates the matter.
However, the death of a major sympathetic character at the end of
Act II indicated the shocking quality of both dramaturgy and theme.
Johnston never has to make a character lecture to the audience that
'Attention must be paid'.

The third act tidies up, as all third acts do, the loose ends of what
will happen to the characters; then it goes on to the central thematic
debate between Tausch and Dobelle, with Dobelle unconventionally but convincingly winning. What the debate is about has now
become more than practicality versus idealism; it is now the proper
definition of right and wrong. Indeed, in noting how right causes
such pain and opting therefore for wrong, Dobelle sounds very like
Dick Dudgeon, Shaw's Devil's Disciple.

A great difference between Shaw and Johnston is that Shaw's right
and wrong, which are usually quite the opposite of society's, are
defined and clear, but Johnston's are not. Tausch stands for reason,
practicality and industrial progress, but he also stands for a love of
art, of family, of humanity and for a kind of idealism. Dobelle stands
for impracticality, for the status *ante quo* and for industrial regress,
but also for a logic beyond practicality as well as for selfishness and
a lack of human sympathy. The issues, as in life, are not clearcut;
the argument, therefore, is a little more complicated than the usual
stage plot-argument. That plot-argument has basically a simple three-
part structure: boy meets girl, boy loses girl, boy gets girl; or John
Wayne knocks Ward Bond down, Ward Bond knocks John Wayne
down, John Wayne knocks Ward Bond out.

In such a simple argument, the plot would be over after the
Tausch-Dobelle debate, and all the playwright would then have to
do would be to construct a quick and effective curtain. In *The Moon,*
however, the statement is not yet completed, and so the plot must
have two more convolutions. When that master of structure, Ben
Jonson, handles a conventional plot as in *Volpone,* he sat Right and
Wrong on opposite ends of a seesaw. One was up and now the

other; and, as the play progressed, the seesaw went faster and faster until Wrong was finally knocked off. In *The Moon,* after Idealism has been totally defeated by Blake's death, it unexpectedly and startlingly wins when the powerhouse is blown up by a comic fluke. The comedy is necessary as a dramaturgic antidote to the previous debate, but it also keeps the triumph of idealism from being sentimental and mawkish.

Sentimentality and mawkishness are charges that have been levelled at the very ending of the play. After the destruction of the powerhouse has cleared most of the actors from the stage and completed the major public action, Dobelle's daughter Blanaid wakes up and comes sleepily down the stairs. Dobelle sees with a start that she resembles his dead wife, and for the first time extends his sympathy and kindness. This is a necessary development for Johnston's theme; Dobelle has intellectually won and presumably converted the audience, but his intellectuality is cold and selfish. For his conversion of the audience to be complete, he himself must be converted by and leavened with the audience's humanity. In staging, this abrupt about-face must be extraordinarily well done, for it has little psychological preparation, and has certainly seemed in poor stagings to be the author prostituting himself for an upbeat ending. Thematically, though, the action is integral; and well staged it could work most touchingly.

The very final scene is simply a coda or dying fall which re-emphasizes the statement about human sympathy and the value of the race. Dobelle and Blanaid have dropped off to sleep. The comic servant, Agnes, having successfully delivered the offstage baby, enters and opens the curtains. The sun comes up. This is all conventional enough, trite even, but a good deal of necessary and effective dramaturgy is trite.

This, I believe, is how the basic structure of the play works and what the play generally says. A full discussion of Johnston's dramaturgy would have to go through the play scene by scene, if not speech by speech and word by word, to point out the utility of everything. In a production, such a weighing and evaluation happen during rehearsal. In criticism, except in rare and enormous instances, there is neither the time nor the space for such close evaluation.

However, as one symptomatic instance of Johnston's thorough-going care for structure, we might contemplate the first short scene of the play to see what it does and why it is there. If we decide that the first scene lasts until Agnes's final exit, there are only about twelve speeches; and yet in them Johnston quickly and firmly establishes the basic comic mode of the play and the strategy of the whole act.

At rise, the girl, Blanaid, is sitting in the window seat reading. She has a couple of actions but no lines. There is also the occasional sound of offstage typing. Agnes is laying the table and has an opening soliloquy which introduces the scene's two jokes. The first is about the suffering of women, as instanced by a neighbour's imminent childbirth (and the announcement of the birth is the appropriate symbolic content of the play's last scene). The second joke is the dramatization of Agnes's cavalier attitude towards her job. The first joke is summed up by the line, 'God knows it's a terrible thing to be a woman'. The second joke is repeated with variations throughout the scene. First, Agnes ignores the knock by saying 'That was a knock at the door', and then continuing what she is doing. When the knock is repeated, she starts to answer it, but stops to talk some more about Mrs Mulpeter's birth pains. Then the knock comes a third time, and Agnes finally answers it with the shout, 'Are you the ignorant bosthoon that's banging and hammering away at my knocker?' This response is so nicely comic that Johnston repeats it by giving Agnes two more short speeches of berating the visitor before exiting with 'Ttt-ttt-ttt! Shocking, shocking!' That line punches her exit and works both as comic sympathy for Mrs Mulpeter and comic irateness against the visitor.

Catching the audience at curtain-rise is difficult in the commercial theatre where for the first five minutes latecomers are pushing through the aisles, locating their seats and treading on people's toes. What is needed dramaturgically is something arresting onstage, something to dissipate the audience's distraction, something big, broad and catchy enough to be repeated. This Johnston adroitly gives, as at the same time he raises the question of who is knocking. Also he leaves two bridges to the following scenes, the silent Blanaid and the offstage typewriter. Each speech and each line of his opening seem defensible as adding either to the comic effect or to the audience's curiosity; and the scene is effectively concluded by Agnes's exit lines which summarize her eccentricity, and emphasized by the bewildered reaction of the visitor. If the visitor's bewilderment is visually broad, the bewildered audience will laugh at his confusion which is more stupid than theirs, while awaiting interestedly the answers to its own questions.

The Moon is a most tightly written play. If the acts are chopped up into the — in the French sense — scenes, nearly each detail of each scene will be found to have its utility.

The use of Agnes to open the play is sound dramaturgy because she is the most conventional of the comic characters, and interest

will be built by the introduction later of successively more engaging
and kookier characters. Some of them are, like Agnes, what one
might call anti-stereotypes. A stereotyped servant would be efficient,
practical, diffident and self-effacing, as well as quite accepting his
lower position in the social order and his lesser importance for the
audience. As an anti-stereotype, Agnes is funny because she
contradicts all of the qualities which the audience expects, and we
laugh, therefore, at the incongruity. The anti-stereotype of the
servant has been a fixture of comic writing from Greek comedy to
Wodehouse; and Johnston's Irish variant is no particularly original
creation. Some of his other anti-stereotypes are more original, but
the originality paradoxically stems from their being counterpointed
to our traditional expectations.

The character of Aunt Columba is somewhat different. She is a
variation of a stereotype. She is in the play because, like all of the
characters, she has a necessity for the development of the theme and
plot. She is in the play also for the comic value of her stereotype
which is that of the decayed spinster, of which literature has many
examples – Hepzibah Pyncheon, the Hon. Impulsia Gushington,
etc., etc. She is crusty and dotty but basically kind. Her comic value
stems from the variations of dottiness that Johnston has invented
for her. Much to his credit, she stays just this side of the absurd.
The story of her one failed love affair, in its details about the wedding gift of the mowing machine, is just within the bounds of
plausibility. Johnston's imaginative detais are never quite farcical
but always fanciful, and yet jibe with Columba's basic stereotype.

The last woman in the cast, Blanaid, is more delicately detailed
and an interesting mixture of stereotype and anti-stereotype. As the
stereotype of the young girl, she is quiet, shy, sensitive and pain-
fully desirous for her father to love her. By themselves, such
characteristics would only make her a bland and usual role that could
figure in a run-of-the-mill romance. Against such stereotypical
characteristics, however, Johnston counterpoints two contradictory,
anti-stereotypical ones – an over-sophistication and an over-naiveté.
Both qualities, in themselves and in juxtaposition, cause not laughter,
but gentle and charmed amusement. Consider, for instance her
early speech to Tausch:

I think that every girl needs an education nowadays in order to prepare her
for the battle of life. She wants to be taught deportment and geography
and religious knowledge and – oh – mathematics. I adore mathematics,
don't you?

The word choice here, a blend of sophistication and naiveté, is finely done. And as much of the comedy is broad, this gentle charm is a welcome contrast and also an indication of Johnston's range.

It would be tediously obvious to investigate every character, to explain why he is necessary for plot or theme, and to analyze his comic characteristics. However, one character, Dobelle, must be looked at.

If the play has a lead, it is Dobelle. His was the part that Claude Rains took in New York and Esme Percy in London. He is the most intelligent character, the one who wins the debate, and the one who changes and grows. Nevertheless, Dobelle is also a borrowing: he is Hamlet, he is the Misanthrope and, above all, he is the Shavian teacher whom we have seen in Sidney Trefusis, Owen Jack, Jack Tanner, Caesar and even Henry Higgins. The Shavian teacher is right, or for the most part right, but Shaw was clever enough to give that rightness some wrongness, some flaws, eccentricities and engaging warts. Dobelle lacks such theatrically Shavian panache, but perhaps just for that reason he comes closer to reality than do Shaw's theatrical characters.

Some commentators thought that Johnston's characterizations were richly, thickly observed renderings of reality. None is; they are all theatrical and with theatrical antecedents. I mean this in no pejorative sense, for Johnston was not writing case studies or Dreiserian novels, but theatre. His characters, even Dobelle, are larger than life. If they are not as monstrously theatrical as Falstaff or Micawber or Tanner, they are quite distinctly of that memorable but unreal breed. In short, once again Johnston's originality has roots in conventionality.

Johnston's fine workmanship is nowhere more apparent than in his language, which too is a consummate use of theatrical convention. To take an obvious example, many of the characters speak in different dialects – Agnes in Moore Street Dublinese, Tausch in Germanic English, George in a breezy Anglo-Irish which is contrasted with the Cockney of his pal, Captain Potts. Dialect has always been a prime device of the comic writer. The quaint divergences of pronunciation and diction of an Irishman, a Scotsman, a Welshman, or a black man from some norm of civilised speech are a source of critical laughter from the audience, as well as a shortcut to characterization.

Most of the traditional linguistic ways of getting laughs have their examples in the play: there is the semi-malapropism, as in George's rendition of Tausch's name as 'Splosch'. This seems stupid on the page, but a lot of passable theatrical humour is stupid on the page;

the answer, of course, is that it belongs not on the page but in the theatre. The 'Splosch' joke is worked several times, and is, like Agnes and the knock at the door, what might be called a 'running gag'. There are about ten running gags in the play, and the utility of the device is evidenced in its popularity in hundreds of comedies — even in *Charley's Aunt* with its famous dumb line, 'I'm from Brazil where the nuts come from'.

If the repetition of 'Splosch' seems low on a scale of humour, it should be noted that Johnston's scale runs from nonsense to wit. One can find examples of half-puns, puns, allusions, inverted clichés, anecdotal jokes, that flip near-wit which might be called banter, and that hallmark of wit which is called the epigram.

To give a handful of examples; there is a half-pun in George's 'This gun is what we call a muzzle-loading, four-inch-slow-firing-Potts-shot. Now explain, Potts.' From the half-pun of 'potshot', we might turn to a full pun in Act III. Tausch has been trying to phone the Minister to relate what has happened, but is interrupted by the explosion, and Dobelle picks up the phone to ask, 'Did the Minister get the report?' There is a nice bit of nonsense in this exchange between Blanaid and Willie:

BLANAID. What were they talking about?
WILLIE. They didn't say, miss.

There is a good use of the inverted cliché in this exchange between Columba and George:

AUNT. . . . Been drowning your troubles in drink, I suppose, as usual.
GEORGE. No, but we've been giving them a damn good swimming lesson.

Dobelle is fond of paradox, such as 'The Will of the People is a tender delicate bloom to be nurtured by the elect few who know best. The icy blasts of a general election are not for it.' Some of Dobelle's best paradoxes and epigrams are invigorated by figurative language. For instance, his, 'Here by the waters of Lethe we may believe in fairies, but we trade in pigs'.

As one might expect from the author of *The Old Lady,* the play contains many allusions, most of them ironically used. After Lanigan's defence of his killing of Blake, he goes off and Dobelle remarks, 'The Moor has done his work. The Moor may go.' A good deal of the writing is, like this, fairly subtle for the stage. Sometimes instead of allusions, one gets what one might call reminiscences. For instance, Dobelle's line, '. . . take away this cursed gift of laughter and give us tears instead', is reminiscent of Juno's most famous line.

(As a matter of fact, Captain Potts has some points of resemblance
to Captain Boyle.) As yet another example of deft but unobtrusive
word finagling, note the following exchange between Dobelle and
Tausch.

DOBELLE. . . . That leaves just you and I.
TAUSCH. I agree. Yes. Just you and me.

Tausch's tacit correction of Dobelle's grammar is a marvellous minor
touch to condemn the correct formality of Tausch's own character.
Or note how in Act I Blanaid's charming ignorance is quietly suggested by a mistake she makes. After telling Dobelle that she was
born in Germany, she mentions that the town was Bratislav.

There is no end of quoting from the many devices in Johnston's
thickly embroidered dialogue; but one last device might be mentioned
because it is unusual, dangerous and successful. I have in mind the
comic anecdote which has nothing whatsoever to do with the plot.
There is at least one anecdote in each act — the story about shooting
the horse has already been cited — and each anecdote stays just
perilously this side of the silly. But it is not merely the nature of
the anecdotes, but even the actual telling of them that is dangerous.
Telling a joke is really for social conversation and not for theatre,
because in a theatre the expectation is that one will not be told jokes
but shown them. Johnston's jokey anecdotes, especially the one
about the drowning of Mrs. Potts, are so fancifully bizarre, however,
that they succeed in enchanting.

I have spent so much time in cataloguing Johnston's devices of
dialogue, that it must be obvious that I think his dialogue one of
the fine points of the play. However, Johnston makes fine use of
the audience's eyes as well as ears. He puts what the audience sees
to sound melodramatic use in the hypnotic clock of Act II; he puts
what the audience sees to simultaneously melodramatic and comic
use when Columba hides the last shell from the police by covering
it with that incongruous item of domestic utility, a tea cosy. He uses
what the audience sees with good farcical effect when Willie drops
the explosive shell, catches it, drops it again, and catches it again,
as the other characters throw themselves on the floor or freeze in
petrified horror. He uses farcical effect when George and Potts tap
a shell with a hammer to see why it has not exploded, or when Willie
does a semi-pratfall as he pushes the gun offstage.

In sum, even in this unsystematic and superficial catalogue of
dramaturgic devices, I have hardly touched upon the variousness,
the soundness and the multiplicity of what Johnston has done.

One wants to cite his consummate comic reversal (see the melodramatic and farcical scene of the masked gunman, Willie, being berated by his mother, Agnes, and finally being pushed to complain piteously that she should not be so violent). One wants to cite. . . .

Nevertheless, perhaps enough points have been cited to indicate that *The Moon in the Yellow River* could be used as a source-book of technique. My real point, however, is that the technique is traditional, and I mean the term totally in admiration. Despite all of the natter about the necessity for new forms and for new experiments, and despite Johnston's own reputation as an experimenter, the theatre in general and his theatre in particular is a stronghold of tradition. That is the theatre's strength, and that is Johnston's strength and the best hope for the survival of his plays upon the stage.

Bad playwrights, ordinary playwrights, boulevard playwrights all exploit the theatre's traditions, but they exploit them poorly. Johnston has exploited them brilliantly. If that has kept him off the stage, it may also in years to come put him on it. That is what happens to classics.

TRYING TO LIKE BECKETT

Well, I suppose I must be wrong, but I do think he is an awful bore. I realize that hordes of very intelligent people would consider this opinion too stupid to qualify for contempt. After all, he has won the Nobel Prize for Literature, he is taught in the universities, and a couple of dozen of books and hundreds of articles have been admiringly written about him. For instance, one of his most knowledgable critics, John Fletcher, has described him as 'a writer having all the essential simplicity of genius'.[1] After *Waiting for Godot* opened in Paris, Jean Anouilh wrote, '*Godot* is a masterpiece that will cause despair for men in general and for playwrights in particular. I think that the opening night at the Théâtre de Babylon is as important as the opening of Pirandello in 1923, presented by Pitoeff.'[2] After *Godot* opened in London, Harold Hobson wrote:

> In my lifetime there have been three first performances of plays that have deeply influenced for good the course of the English drama. The earliest, and I think the most important of these, was the opening performance at the Arts Theatre on August 3rd, 1955, of Samuel Beckett's *Waiting for Godot*. . . . It revealed that the drama approximates, or can approximate, to the condition of music, touching chords deeper than can be reached by reason, and saying things beyond the grasp of logic. It renewed the English theatre in a single night.[3]

Harold Pinter, quite as enthusiastically wrote, 'He is the most courageous, remorseless writer going, and the more he grinds my nose in the shit the more I am grateful to him . . . he seems to me far and away the finest writer writing.'[4] Ruby Cohn, his most prolific American commentator, wrote, 'The impact of *Godot* is immediate; the impact of *Godot* is inexhaustible. Vaudeville turns are threaded on philosophic nihilism and a classico-Christian tradition. The seed of *Godot* is Luke's account of the Crucifixion, as summarized by St. Augustine. . . .' And elsewhere: 'During the long sickness of his writing life, Beckett has shivered through many a fever to chart a being that is bounded by nothing. Under Beckett's spell, we too come to strain toward nothing — but through densities and immensities.'[5] But perhaps the most overwhelming statement of all is this one by Martin Esslin, the respected author of *The Theatre of the Absurd* and other books:

113

To be in communication with a mind of such merciless integrity, of such uncompromising determination to face the stark reality of the human situation and to confront the worst without even being in danger of yielding to any of the superficial consolations that have clouded man's self-awareness in the past; to be in contact with a human being utterly free from self-pity, utterly oblivious to the pitfalls of vanity or self-glorification, even the most venial complacency of all, the illusion of being able to lighten one's anguish by sharing it with others; to see a lone figure without hope of comfort, facing the great emptiness of space and time without the possibilities of miraculous rescue or salvation, in dignity, resolved to fulfill its obligation to express its own predicament – to partake of such courage and noble stoicism, however remotely, cannot but evoke a feeling of emotional excitement, exhilaration.[6]

And quotations scarcely less effusive, and rather better structured than the last one, could be multiplied a hundredfold. So I utterly must be wrong.

But I still do not like him, and I still think he is an awful bore. In fact, I suspect that the people who like him most are a bit masochistic – high-minded, no doubt, intelligent, deeply serious, but a bit masochistic. Unlike Anouilh, I am not keen about literature that evokes despair. Aesthetically, I do not think too highly of philosophic nihilism and straining toward nothing. And more vulgarly, I am not in the least grateful for having my nose ground in the shit.

Nevertheless, such attitudes are widespread, and Beckett still enjoys a cultural trendiness. We can speak ill of him no more than of Marcel Proust or Thomas Mann or several others of the much admired and little read. The reason for the reputations of Proust or Mann or even that consummate bore Henry James are explicable enough. But Beckett's reputation is probably more than upper-middlebrow snobbery or academic aggrandizement. A clever person like Ruby Cohn strikes me as totally sincere, and one who finds in Beckett the last refuge of an intelligent person of good will in a chaotic and insane world. To the intelligent, aware, sensitive mind, Beckett is probably the most plausible, if most miniscule, affirmation possible in the face of our madly malignant world. Yet there is here a masochistic defeatism that the world's noblest minds have never acquiesced in previously, no matter how hopeless was man's state or man's future.

Beckett is a particularly individual oddball, but he fits the spirit of the times. Deirdre Bair's recent, decent, if much criticised biography does offer a feasible explanation of what kind of oddball; and these briefly are the facts:

He was born Samuel Barclay Beckett on 13 April or 13 May, 1906, in Foxrock, a fashionable suburb of Dublin, into a well-to-do Protestant family. From 1920 to 1923, he attended Portora Royal School in Eniskillen, as had Oscar Wilde before him. In the Fall of 1923, he entered Trinity College, Dublin; and, after a lackluster beginning, he distinguished himself in modern languages and received his B.A. in 1927. He taught for nearly a year in Belfast and then for nearly two years in Paris.

In Paris, he met Thomas McGreevy, the Irish poet and art critic, who introduced him to James Joyce whose later work was unquestionably the strongest influence on Beckett's own writing. For some time, Beckett was closely involved with Joyce and his family, and contributed an essay to the first volume of Joycean apologetics and explication. He also published in the avant garde magazine *transition,* published a conventionally avant garde long poem called *Whoroscope,* and published an Anais Nin-like book on Proust.

In the Fall of 1930, he returned to Dublin to teach at Trinity College, but Ireland, apparently largely because of his demanding mother, made him acutely, physically ill. In December 1931, he received his M. A., and fled back to the Continent.

Beckett's next twenty years were ones of great difficulty. He lived mainly in Paris, but was often drawn back to Dublin by the demands of his family. In 1932, he wrote a still unpublished novel called *Dream of Fair to Middling Women,* and in 1934 he published a collection of stories called *More Pricks than Kicks.* His novel *Murphy* finally appeared in 1938 to relatively little notice after having been refused by more than forty publishers.

During World War II, Beckett was active in the French Resistance in Paris, but was forced to flee in the Fall of 1942 to a village in southeast France. There he remained until 1945, although managing to write his novel *Watt.* After the war he returned to Paris and received the Croix de Guerre for his work in the Resistance.

After the war he entered upon his most productive period. *Molloy,* probably his best novel, was finished in 1948, and quickly followed by *Malone Dies* and by *Waiting for Godot* and *The Unnamable,* all of which were originally written in French. In 1953, *Godot* was produced in Paris to wide acclaim and bafflement, and similar productions followed in London and New York. The play became a topic for excited debate. Here was finally a play that offered the tantalizing ambiguity that the well-read had come to expect in the modern novel and poem. The play's vogue not only established Beckett as an important author, but also cleared the way for a new wave of theatrical experiment by Ionesco, Adamov, Pinter and all those others who were to be classed as dramatists of the Absurd.

After *Godot,* Beckett's other major works were brought into print, and in 1956 he wrote probably his second best known play, *Endgame.* In 1969, he received the Nobel Prize for Literature, and since then he has tended to write more plays than fiction, but all of his pieces have become increasingly more brief.

The greatest influences on Beckett as a writer seem to have been Joyce, Ireland and illness. Beckett met Joyce at an early and impressionable age, when Joyce was writing the most complicated experimental novel in English or probably any other language. The impact of *Finnegans Wake* upon Beckett was profound and lasting. Beckett's other main influences, Ireland and illness, seem quite interconnected. He has been afflicted with an astonishing array of ailments, and his worst symptoms usually seemed brougnt on by a return to Ireland. His catalogue of ills is so extensive that it does much to explain his gallery of enfeebled, debilitated characters and his constant theme of life as a kind of incurable disease. His characters do not really exist in an identifiable Irish landscape, but they do seem maimed refugees from that landscape after someone has dropped an H-bomb on it.

Beckett's works, then, represent experiments in form, which depict an unrealistic world filled with repugnant and pointless details, and which make the point that the real world is repugnant and pointless. Such characteristics would seem unpromising indeed for art, but Beckett has three extraordinary qualities as an experimental writer. First, there is the ingenious, often comic objectification that he finds for his world-view. The details of *Molloy* and *Godot* and *Endgame* create a much more austere world than those of Lewis Carroll or William Faulkner, but quite as individual a one. The details of these fairly early works are so engaging, so dourly droll, that to some extent they defeat the author's purpose and actually entertain an audience. In his later, 'purer' works, he keeps a much tighter rein upon his comic invention.

Second, there is the quality of his prose which, phrase by phrase and sentence by sentence, has a quite unJoycean simplicity and clarity. In *Finnegans Wake,* Joyce is the great 'accretor,' piling nuance upon nuance, until the density of meaning defies conventional reading and demands translation. Beckett goes almost to the other extreme. His prose is always lucid and fluent, and never quirky or idiosyncratic, as the simple styles of Gertrude Stein or Ernest Hemingway sometimes become. Beckett's prose is always a clear mirror of his content.

Third, there is Beckett's attempt to wrench his form into an emphasis of his statement, and this attempt is both his most daring and his least successful. A not always true 'truism' of aesthetics is that form should emulate, or at least emphasize, content. Certainly, form can sometimes do that, and one can cite innumerable instances in modern literature, from Walt Whitman on. However, a rigid form like a Shakespearean sonnet, for instance, suggests nothing except a certain pattern of reasoning; yet into that form poets have poured a multitude of diverse meanings and emotions.

Beckett, by rigidly molding form to content, has at his most Beckettian broken the mold. Someone has said that *Waiting for Godot* is a play in which nothing happens twice. That same point can be made about many of Beckett's other works. The Moran portion of *Molloy* is basically a reprise of the Molloy portion. The second half of the play, entitled *Play,* repeats the first half verbatim, the only difference being that Beckett thinks that the second half should be done more hesitantly. The 'Dramaticule' called *Come and Go* in its scant ten minutes repeats the same unengaging action three times. The play *Breath* in its thirty-five or forty seconds repeats its initial action in reverse. The only difference in these works is that Beckett succeeds in being boring in an ever shorter period of time.

'Boring' is really too innocuous a word. As Beckett's world-view is of an intolerable existence which it is not worthwhile terminating, the appropriate Beckettian form is necessarily a worthless one, an anti-form. Such a form evokes neither emotion nor amusement; it passes the time at worst tediously and at best intolerably. Increasingly over the years, Beckett seems to have refined that form, to have stripped it of details, and to have made it more austere. He has used fewer words and even no words; he has used fewer actors, parts of actors, and even no actors.

In the theatre, there is no question that Beckett's form emulates his meaning; but there is the question of how valid the effect of his form is upon an audience. In 1960,when Cyril Cusack consummately played *Krapp's Last Tape* as an afterpiece rather than as a curtain-raiser to Shaw's *Arms and the Man,* he succeeded in half-emptying the Queen's Theatre of an up-to-then highly appreciative audience. In 1967 when the Abbey mounted a very fine production of *Play,* the audience was respectfully attentive for the first half, but increasingly restive and whispering when the dialogue was run through again. And, if it had been run through a third time, I am certain that most of the audience would have been outside in the foyer. That may, of course, have been the effect Beckett wanted. The effect would not be dramatic but it would be memorable. Similarly, one could fire off a cannon during a Shakespearean production at the Globe Theatre; and, when the theatre burns down, the effect is extremely memorable, even though the dramatic experiment has destroyed the form of the drama.

In other words, Beckett's plays work in the way that he wants them to, but they do not work as plays, and I cannot like them as plays. One may use a Rolls-Royce as a quite effective chicken coop, but in that function it can hardly be admired as a Rolls-Royce. Indeed, a Rolls-Royce functioning as a chicken coop would seem a rather melancholy object and a sadly debased one. To me, a Beckett play on the stage seems a similar debasement of a noble form. A debasement and a perversion.

To a conventional or traditional view of what literature can do, it would seem that Beckett's most successful works are those in which he has been less Beckettian. In this view, the works — *Murphy, Molloy* and *Endgame,* and to some extent *Malone Dies* and *Godot* — would appear to be the works by which Beckett will be remembered. In these works, his subsequently, and I think purposely, stifled comic imagination is brilliantly apparent. While that comic imagination may work against the author's intention, it triumphantly works for the traditional methods of the artist.

SINCE O'CASEY

I

The major trend of Irish drama today is toward extinction. I do not mean that Irishmen have stopped writing plays; there is a lot of writing and some of it fine. What is dying is not the drama in Ireland, but the drama of Ireland. And the reason is simply that the Irishness of Ireland is everyday being rapidly dissipated. A few years ago I was commissioned to do a television play about Ireland. I did not envision my players standing in front of Celtic crosses or holy wells or the lakes of Killarney, as did my wife's grandfather, James Mark Sullivan, when he sent people out to make an Irish film in 1916. My characters were leaning against an automobile, and in the sky behind them was the metallic arm of a crane in the process of knocking down a Georgian house and erecting an office slab of steel and glass.

I have been a close Ireland-watcher since 1960. Then, when I first saw Dublin, I was struck by three qualities — the basic eighteenth century nobility of the place, the bleakly Hard Times nineteenth century squalor of it, and the abruptly twentieth century proliferation of television antennas. The country was just then on the verge of a violent acceleration into modern times, and that acceleration was neatly symbolised by the skeleton of a TV antenna attached to a collapsing chimney pot.

One could still see what O'Casey's first plays had been written about; one could even see the older, statelier presence of Conal O'Riordan's novels. But since then all is changed, changed unutterably.[1] The small provision shop is being replaced by the supermarket. The once charming road from Dublin to Greystones is in some danger of becoming an urban sprawl. The traffic through College Green is no longer mainly composed of girls riding bicycles and trying to say the Rosary with one hand while holding down their skirts with the other. The traffic is automobiles and too many of them. The film censorship has much relaxed; while Joseph Holloway as Deputy Film Censor once made a cut in *Snow White and the Seven Dwarfs,* one could now view items like *Super Vixens* or *The Bitch.* The book censorship has allowed at least marshmellow pornography into the country; *Playboy* is still not allowed, but Ireland publishes its own bare-breasted equivalent. The notion that sex can be fun rather than functional also emerged in the recent ridiculous – but until recently quite unthinkable – public compromise about contraception. In sum, the effects of the Lemass government's encouragement of foreign investment, of Vatican II's weakening of clerical influence, of Ireland's active participation in the U.N. and of its entrance into the E.E.C., have all been pervasive and profound.

In the 1950s, O'Casey's late plays were still anathema. There was much public criticism and mild public demonstrations when Cyril Cusack produced *The Bishop's Bonfire* in the Gaiety in 1955. There was much private influence and much private fear that impelled the withdrawal of *The Drums of Father Ned* from the second Dublin Theatre Festival in 1958. However, those were the last days of de Valera's uptight little island, and it was that little island that O'Casey's late works savaged. In the 1960s and 1970s, most of O'Casey's late plays have been produced in Ireland, and often by the national theatre, and often to considerable acclaim. Of course, the reason simply was that what O'Casey had savaged no longer basically existed.

In the last twenty years, the pre-occupations of Irishmen have considerably changed. The desires, the interests and the tastes of Irishmen have become much less distinguishable from those of modern man in America or England or France or anywhere. For immensely better or deplorably worse, the twentieth century has seen the growth of an amorphous mass culture; and the last twenty years have seen that growth envelop Ireland. Individual national differences have become increasingly minimised. Mass marketing of Southern Fried Chicken, of James Bond and of Toyotas has evolved a supra-national similarity everywhere.

Of course, some things change more slowly; and in Ireland two of the most stable things are relative poverty and small productivity. That fact, combined with more ambitious materialistic desires, has resulted in a constant series of strikes, even in such masochistically basic areas as banking, transportation, communications[2] and even the burial of the dead.

One other notable, if dubiously widespread, stability is the matter of nationalism. About a dozen years ago, this hideous spectre raised its vicious head in the North, and has since resulted in more than two thousand deaths and inestimable civil disruption. In 1968, the man in the street had become the man in the Morris Minor, and he was more interested in trading upward to a Mercedes than in trading insults, or bombs and bullets, with Britain. At first, this patriotic anachronism, in its most intense IRA embodiment,

seemed only the usual activity of the small lunatic fringe. But, as
the Northern turmoil was also fuelled by unemployment and
frustration and boredom, it has stubbornly refused to dissipate; and
to some extent it has revived the old dormant feelings of 'A Nation
Once Again'. The 1980-81 hunger strikes brought hundreds of
demonstrators out onto the streets in well stage-managed demonstrations, including a nasty one in the summer of 1981 near the British
Embassy in Ballsbridge.

Nevertheless, despite some persuasive evidence, I do not think that
the nationalistic impulse is as central to the Irish psyche as it was
sixty or a hundred years ago. I think that this last, tenacious
embodiment of it has its tap root embedded less in patriotism than
in economics and hopelessness. Artistically, at any rate, it is now
impossible to turn back to the Nationalism of *Kathleen ni Houlihan*
or even of *The Rising of the Moon*. If a playwright makes a human
generalization today, does the Irishman cast it in O'Casey's slums,
or the Russian in Gorky's, or the Spaniard in Lorca's villages? More
probably the playwright takes a French heroine, puts her in a comic
strip Chicago, and calls the melange *St. Joan of the Stockyards*. Or
Friel and Kilroy transplant Chekhov to Ireland. Obviously this is
a generalization with exceptions, yet it seems to me an unexcep-
tionable generalization.

Other than overt nationalism, the two major themes of the hey-
day of the dramatic renaissance were the heroic past and the peasant present. Today, the heroic past can only be used for grotesque
or comic purposes, as in the enchanting whimseys of Flann
O'Brien.[2] And the peasant has now moved to Dublin or
Manchester or Philadelphia; John Murphy's Country Boy has been
superseded by Edna O'Brien's Country Girl who left the farm, threw
away her bra (she never had a shift), and did not look back.

There is still much fine drama written in Ireland and set in Ireland,
but its Irishness is dissipated, and its Oirishness is, thank God,
decayed, defunct, dead. There are some current writers with the talent
to create a Joxer Daly for today, but none of them has, and the
reason is that a modern Joxer would be as strange and untrue as
a brontosaurus. Even O'Casey's late, best, brilliant characters –
Codger Sleehaun, Skerighan the Ulsterman, Angela and Lizzie –
already belong to history. Brian Friel's Ireland, Thomas Murphy's
and Eugene McCabe's, Thomas Kilroy's and John B. Keane's and
James Douglas's, is an Ireland in transition; and when Hugh Leonard
writes seriously of Ireland, he writes of his boyhood in Dalkey
thirty golden years ago. Some of the finest new plays look back
nostalgically to the Ireland of yesterday, as does Friel's *Aristocrats;*

but the characters of the play, and of *The Savages,* and of *The Sanctuary Lamp,* and of *Cancer,* and of *Tea and Sex and Shakespeare* are all men of the modern world who happen to live in the country cailed Ireland.

I think it is wrong to mourn the passing of something we only thought we loved. That notion of Ireland is like our notion of the lover we lost — glamourised, idealised, marvellous and false. The works of genius by Synge and Yeats and Lady Gregory and Fitzmaurize and O'Casey bedazzled us. But it is no treachery to that old bedazzlement to be enchanted by the fine European writers in Ireland today.

II

The Irish stage, or any commercial stage, is primarily geared to entertainment. The reason is that the stage is a business; and, to be a successful business, the stage must please.

In this century in Dublin, the most popular pieces have been items like *The Private Secretary, Charley's Aunt* and *Chu Chin Chow.* Or, more recently, *The Boy Friend, My Fair Lady* and *Annie.* Or, to take the Irish entertainments, it has been Christmas pantos and summer revues with Jimmy O'Dea or Maureen Potter or Jack Cruise; it has been the Rathmines and Rathgar Musical Society doing Gilbert and Sullivan or *Mauritana* or *The Bohemian Girl* or *The Merry Widow;* it has been patriotic melodramas at the old Queen's and *Professor Tim* and his ilk at the old Abbey.

Take one typical year — take, say 1972 because I was in a minor way involved in it. That year saw more than simply entertainment. Tom Murphy's *The White House* was first staged at the Abbey, and there were also revivals of O'Casey's *The Silver Tassie,* Friel's *Philadelphia, Here I Come!,* Shaw's *St. Joan,* O'Neill's *The Iceman Cometh* and even, although hardly a work of art, of the hardy *Arrah na Pogue* of Boucicault. The new plays at the Peacock included Behan's *Richard's Cork Leg* and Magee's *Hatchet,* as well as new pieces by Tom MacIntyre and Eugene McCabe. At the Eblana there was James Douglas's *The Savages,* and at the Gate there was Desmond Forristal's first play, *The True Story of the Horrid Popish Plot.* In retrospect, not a bad year at all for the serious drama.

Nevertheless, what drew the most audiences were an English melodrama, a comic review, a Christmas pantomime and the above-mentioned musical farce by Behan. The melodrama was *Sleuth* in an Irish production directed by Godfrey Quigley and starring Donal Donnelly and T. P. McKenna. It ran for ten weeks at the Olympia, the largest theatre in town, with a seating capacity of about 1500; and it packed out, making, according to my reliable informants, somewhere in the vicinity of £40,000. Ten weeks is no run in America, but it is superb for Dublin with its much smaller audience. Similarly, £40,000 was theatrical peanuts for New York, but in 1972 it approached caviar for Dublin. *Sleuth* succeeded in Dublin for the same reason that it did in London and New York. It is a cleverly constructed thriller with opportunities for bravura acting, and its audiences left the theatre with a comfortable placidity which is not to be undervalued.

The comic revue, *Sweet and Sour,* played at the small, depressing Eblana Theatre for about eight months. Its material was feeble and the show is now quite forgotten, but its three actors − Maureen Toal, Anna Manahan and Des Keogh − played it with so much dash that its audiences ambled away, if not enthralled, at least momentarily entertained. The Christmas pantomime at the Gaiety as usual starred Maureen Potter. Also as usual the script appealed to very small children and rather backward adults, but its diminutive star is so dynamic a singer, a dancer and a comedienne that audiences gratefully, as they have for years, filled the Gaiety to see her.

Richard's Cork Leg was the play that Brendan Behan was tinkering with at his death, and which was thought to exist only in miniscule fragments written on the backs of old cigarette packs. Mrs. Behan unearthed enough of the script, however, to give to Alan Simpson, the original producer of *The Quare Fellow.* Simpson completed the play and staged one of his inimitably lively productions, with a cast of Abbey actors rounded out by the popular ballad singers, the Dubliners. The Dubliners are not actors, but their Ronnie Drew and Luke Kelly were good enough, and they sang rousingly. And of the Abbey actors, Joan O'Hara as one of the whores gave an unforgettable farcical performance. The piece proved to be vintage Behan, full of songs, shaggy dog stories, scruffy old jokes and amusing language. Despite being a bit dated and despite some mordant moments, it delighted immensely. It was good enough to move to the Olympia and then to London where, despite the Ulster horror, it did fairly well. I saw it three times with growing enchantment.

These were the good entertainments, but can a serious play aspiring to more than simple entertainment be as successful as a tuneful musical, a broad farce or a well-crafted mystery melodrama? Sometimes it can, but not probably on its own intrinsic merits. It needs help. In 1972, I had a play at the Gate which was seriously intended, seriously received and well attended. Indeed, people were turned away, and the first week of the engagement broke the box-office records of the theatre − but despite all of that, the play wound up slightly in the red. The reason for the play's popularity was not, I am afraid, its intrinsic excellence, but that the audience expected glamour and titillation. The glamour came from the first appearance of a movie star, Lynn Redgrave, on a Dublin stage; and the management could possibly have done as well if she had done no more than stood on a bare stage and read *Gorboduc* in Hungarian. The titillation came from the expectation of seeing a dirty play. The mixed notices, which ranged from 'an adult play, remorselessly explicit, of much subtlety and accomplishment' to 'Vulgar, sordid and offensive', were all money notices, inasmuch as they suggested that what was going on at the Gate Theatre was pretty hot stuff. My sad, sour little piece was so far from being hot stuff that − . Ah well, what brings people into the theatre, in Ireland or anyplace else, is the expectation of some bovine razzle-dazzle.

Or, to take another example of a serious play that was pretty commercially successful: in May 1977, Edwards and Mac Liammóir presented *Equus* at the Gate. This was a serious play of some intellectual pretensions by Peter Shaffer, the brother of the *Sleuth* author. Shaffer's play had had long runs in London and New York, and was made into a Richard Burton movie. For Dublin, the daring of the performance was that there were occasionally a couple of naked bodies on the stage, one of them a young male. This incident, which would have been unthinkable very few years earlier, passed off quite without furor of any kind, and the play achieved for Dublin a very good run.

Equus is not a great play, but it poses a unique situation, investigates with some subtlety a serious theme, and contains − particularly in the staging of the horses − some eminently theatrical elements. The play came to Dublin with an established reputation as a serious contemporary drama, and its nude scenes were staged with something amounting to reverence; the content of the play and the whole ambience of the production insisted that the nudity was essential stuff in a rather sombre cultural experience. Well and good, and the forces of puritanism held off. The audiences packed the theatre, though, and one reason was certainly the nudity on stage which could be viewed without the onus of being thought a peeping tom.

In other words, a serious play needs more than its own intrinsic excellence to succeed commercially. *Waiting for Godot* with Peter O'Toole is going to do much better business than *Waiting for Godot* without him.

This is a truism applicable to the stage of any country. What makes the modern Irish stage a trifle different, however, is that within this

basic milieu of broad public entertainment so many serious plays
have emerged.

III

Nevertheless, the theatre in Dublin, as anywhere else, is always
being strangled by its intolerable economics. The Irish government
for about sixty years has subsidised the Abbey, and to Yeats and
Lady Gregory the present subsidy would seem astronomical. In 1972,
the government began a subsidy for the Gate, and also footed the
bill for the creation of a second national theatre which has been called
the Irish Theatre Company and which presented four productions
a year and spent about twenty-four weeks touring the country.[3]
None of these theatres, even if they sold every seat for every night
of the year, can exist without these public funds.

The Dublin Theatre Festival, which had one of its best years in
1980, is still the annual showcase of what presumably is the best of
the newest work being done. Over the years, the Festival has come
in for much criticism, but it has done some fine work and has always
generated such interest that no one could possibly argue for its
abolishment.[3] However, despite selling a high percentage of its
tickets, the Festival could not exist without large subsidies from the
Tourist Board, the Guinness Brewery and any other source that does
not mind losing money. But even with such subsidies, the history
of the Festival has always been dotted with recurring financial crises,
and its immediate future is at the moment problematical.

Economics is the ruling force in the Irish theatre, even for the subsidized houses. In modern times, theatre has almost always been
primarily a business. The Globe Theatre produced an extraordinary
number of masterpieces, but *Hamlet* would never have reached the
boards unless the theatre had made money. Molière's troupe, the
Drury Lane of Garrick and Sheridan, innumerable companies during the nineteenth century headed by leading actors, and even the
Moscow Arts Theatre, the Abbey, the Provincetown Playhouse, the
Group Theatre, the Old Vic, the Theater Guild, the Playwrights'
Company, the English National Theatre, the Public Theater of
Joseph Papp — these and dozens more have all been, no matter what
their estimable intentions or brilliant accomplishments, fundamen-
tally, finally, businesses.

The theatre as business must succeed as business. Unless a theatre
finally at least breaks even, whether by success or subsidy, its doors
will close; and there will be no *Hamlet,* no *Tartuffe,* no *School*

for Scandal, no *Juno and the Paycock.*

This inexorable fact has profound influence on what the theatre produces. If a producing company has nothing to lose, it may take chances. That is, if the company is a group of young people trying to make an impact, producing for peanuts, playing on some postage-stamp stage in a basement or back alley, then chances may — indeed, must — be taken. But if the company has a lot to lose — an investment, a debt, a playhouse, a standing company of actors and technicians to be paid — then it has to play it cool, to be cautious, to take few chances.

In the theatre, caution is the inevitable by-product of success; and success must be defined as a precarious, all too temporary stability. Caution means mainly that the new productions will be those most likely to bring people to the box-office. In Ireland, as in London or New York, caution specifically means that about five kinds of plays will be staged: those which are like previously successful plays, those which are by previously successful playwrights, those revivals which were previously successful, those importations which were strong successes in London or New York, and adaptations of successful works from other media.

Let us consider just the matter of adaptations which have traditionally been among the safest choices. In nineteenth century England and America, there were the innumerable adaptations of Scott and Dickens; and high among the most played plays of the century were the several pieces adapted from Mrs. Henry Wood's weepy novel *East Lynne* and Harriet Beecher Stowe's sentimental and melodramatic tract *Uncle Tom's Cabin.*

In recent Ireland, there seem to have been almost as many adaptations as original plays. From 1966 to 1976, just the Abbey alone offered, and sometimes revived, these: a scissors and paste job by Tomás Mac Anna and Edward Golden called *Recall the Years,* P. J. O'Connor's adaptation of Kavanagh's novel *Tarry Flynn,* Frank McMahon's adaptation of Behan's memoir *Borstal Boy,* Mary Manning's adaptation of Frank O'Connor's novel *The Saint and Mary Kate,* Sally Miles's adaptation of The Wakefield Mystery Plays, Tomás Mac Anna's adaptation of Father O'Leary's *Seadna,* P. J. O'Connor's adaptation of Eric Cross's sketches *The Tailor and Ansty,* Audry Walsh's adaptation of Flann O'Brien's novel *At Swim-Two-Birds,* Marjorie Barkentin's Joycean adaptation called *Ulysses in Nighttown,* Thomas Murphy's adaptation of Goldsmith's *The Vicar of Wakefield,* and Fergus Linehan's and Jim Doherty's musical adaptation of Lennox Robinson's *Drama at Inish.* Downstairs in the Peacock, the Abbey presented during the same period

Sean Ó Briain's adaptation of Myles's *An Beal Bocht,* the O'Connor *Tarry Flynn,* a revival of Lady Gregory's adaptation of Molière's *The Doctor in Spite of Himself,* a scissors and paste job called *The Soung of the Gong* by Linehan and Mac Anna, O'Connor's *Tailor and Ansty,* Micheál Ó hAodha's adaptation of Seumas O'Kelly's story *The Weaver's Grave,* Walsh's *At Swim-Two-Birds,* a scissors and paste job by Mac Anna and Eugene Watters called *A State of Chassis,* G. P. Gallivan's adaptation of the treaty discussions called *The Dail Debates,* Mac Anna's scissors and paste *Dear Edward* after George Moore, Jim Sheridan's Molière adaptation called *The Happy-Go-Lucky Man,* and Pat Layde's adaptation of Flann O'Brien's *The Hard Life.* I may have missed a few.

And, of course, the Gate and the other local companies were adapting almost as prolifically; and I have read or am aware of a score or two of other adaptations that did not reach production.

My own bias is firmly toward original drama, and I basically regard adaptations as a stopgap and a substitute. Nevertheless, one should not be too snotty; after all, many of Shakespeare's finest plays were basically adaptations – from Plutarch or Hollinshed or, in the case of *Hamlet,* from an earlier play. And a handful of these Irish adaptations were among the stronger theatre pieces of the time. I have in mind particularly the McMahon *Borstal Boy* which, with Niall Toibin and Frank Grimes in Mac Anna's fine production, was justly successful in New York; P. J. O'Connor's broad *Tarry Flynn* and his very adroit *Tailor and Ansty,* Mary Manning's enchanting theatrical translation of the picaresque *Saint and Mary Kate,* and several of Hugh Leonard's pieces, especially *Stephen D* and *The Dead* after Joyce, and *When the Saints Go Cycling In* after Flann O'Brien's *The Dalkey Archive.* And there were perhaps a dozen others scarcely less strong.

However, when we add up all of the adaptations, and add them to the imitations, and the new pieces by established writers, and the revivals of old pieces by established writers, and the commercial imports of Neil Simon or the Shaffer brothers, and the musicals, and the rock musicals, and the imitations of rock musicals – then it becomes blindingly apparent that playing it safe leaves very little room for playing it any other way.

It leaves very little room for new plays even by established writers who have never made it as commercially big as have Friel and Leonard – not even for such fine writers as Douglas or Judge or Hayes. Not even for Michael J. Molloy. Unless one runs a theatre, as have the Sheridan brothers at the Project, it leaves very, very little room for the new writer. For every one or two lucky ones, like

Heno Magee or J. Graham Reid or Bernard Farrell, who do break
through, there are six others who do not. And, of course, breaking
through is vastly helped if one has already broken through elsewhere
– published a novel or a book of stories, won a prize, had a play
produced in London or New York.

In New York, there is still Off-Off Broadway for the new
playwright, although economics and Actors' Equity have combined
in the last three years to double production costs (so that even Off-
Off Broadway is playing it cool, and half of its plays are now
revivals). There is no equivalent of Off-Off Broadway in Dublin;
and so, with so few opportunities for production, it is well-nigh amazing that so many new writers continue somehow to appear.

IV

Any account of the playwrights of the last fifteen years must com-
mence with Brian Friel, for he has done more work of the highest
quality than anyone else. Friel is not a technical innovator, but he
remains fascinated by trying out in his basically realistic plays various
non-realistic techniques. The split personality of Public Gar and
Private Gar, played by two actors in *Philadelphia, Here I Come!*
was not original. Eugene O'Neill had done it twenty-five years before
in *Days Without End;* however, Friel handled it with brilliant success, and possibly that success has impelled him to try again. In most
of his later plays, though, the technical device is little more than clut-
ter. The commentators in *Lovers* added little to those adroit short
plays. The sociologist in *The Freedom of the City* and Sir in the much
finer *Living Quarters* contributed little broadening content and mainly just interrupted matters. The American professor in *Aristocrats*
had even less to do and was even more of a bore. As Conor Cruise
O'Brien said of Sir, 'Those Brechtian and post-Brechtian devices that
were supposed to be liberating from the fetters of traditional
dramaturgy are beginning to look suspiciously like fetters themselves.
Putting it another way, Sir is a pain in the neck.' Friel apparently
uses such devices as Shaw used his Prefaces, to broaden and deepen
the statement of the play. But except for the one superb instance
of Private Gar, they just do not carry their weight. They dissipate
the dramatic energy; they are tedious.

Friel is an accomplished technician of conventional plotting, and
that statement is meant in admiration – for conventional plotting
in the modern drama would not only include the most traditional
linear development of a plot such as Friel used in *The Enemy Within,*

and the hurried up version of such a plot that he used most appropriately for the satiric farce, *The Mundy Scheme.* It would also include the tight versions of conventional plotting that Ibsen has taught us and that Friel used in *Living Quarters;* and it would include the complicated tragi-comic structure that Chekhov taught us and that Friel used in *Aristocrats.* With such structural control, Friel hardly needs neo-Expresionistic crutches and neo-Brechtian gimmicks.

In fact, such gimmicks only detract from his real strength which is the depiction of character. Of all of Friel's technical experiments, only the split-personality device in *Philadelphia* and the split-language device in *Translations* worked well. The split-personality device deepened characterization, and the split-language device deepened irony and pathos. All of Friel's other attempts only undramatically, as in a lecture, attempt to expand the theme. However, the plights of the finely drawn characters in *Living Quarters* and *Aristocrats* do not need their plights explained or made more moving. We fully understand and are much moved without any of the gimmicks whatsoever.

To say that Friel's forte is character is dangerous, for the generalizations of critics tend to congeal into clichés from which poor playwrights struggle to escape for years. When Lady Gregory wrote to O'Casey that his early plays indicated that his strong point was character, she did him and his work immeasurable harm. For in *Within the Gates* and *The Star Turns Red* and other plays which he could have written better, O'Casey seemed to bend over backward to prove her wrong.

So, to make my remark less portentous, let me do some qualifying. Friel usually does not try for the Dickensian-O'Caseyan eccentric. He was playing around with such characters of necessity in the broad *Mundy Scheme,* and he perhaps tried more seriously with a broad character in *Cass Maguire.* F. X., the politician of *The Mundy Scheme* is fine for a satiric farce, but a Micawber cannot carry the whole plot of a serious play; and poor Cass Maguire did not even have much of a plot. In his best work, however, Friel does not try for the stock character, although in the seriously intended *The Freedom of the City* he resorted to stock characters in his three leads. The reason seems probably that he was trying for strength of statement. Although *Freedom* is more interesting than the run-of-the-mill thesis play, character does get sacrificed to thesis.

Despite the great success of his beautifully sentimental *Philadelphia,* Friel does not usually try for easy sympathy. In Gar and in the young people of *Lovers,* he has shown that he can consummately evoke emotion; but what makes him interesting is that in his most accomplished later work he tries for something harder than sympathy and colder than tears.

In *Crystal and Fox* of 1968, Friel draws an evocative picture of that lamentably defunct phenomenon, the travelling drama troupe known as the fit-up company. But in Fox, he draws an absorbing portrait of a man who bit by bit dismantles his company and his life. Nowhere in the play does Friel answer with sufficient theatrical clarity the central question posed by the action — why does Fox so inexorably, masochistically do this? And that is the chief failure of the play, that modern short story subtlety that the drama's patrons cannot handle.

I think that Fox does not understand or — as his last marvellous speech indicates — only half-understands his motivations. I think also that Friel is making a sadly Beckettian statement about life, but that he does not make it strongly enough for the audience to get it. What the audience can get is an engrossing two hours, in which they are captivated by a somewhat enigmatic personality whom they cannot entirely like. There is more poignance to be drawn from hardness than from shmarm, and I think the play is almost masterly.

Friel's next real achievement in this kind of character drawing is Commandant Frank Butler of *Living Quarters,* a strong, simple and not very articulate man who cannot finally cope with the inevitable failures of living. For the theatre, he is an unusual conception. With him, we are light years away from Joxer Daly. Perhaps Shakespeare tried such a character in Coriolanus; in the Irish drama, perhaps Walter Macken approached it in the father of *Home Is the Hero,* and John B. Keane approached it in the father of *The Year of the Hiker.* But both Macken and Keane squelched sympathy for their characters, while Friel, with no theatrical simplifications or cajoling fakeries, invites it. About the only other similarly cold character I can think of in Irish drama is Drumm, the hero of Hugh Leonard's *A Life,* a part beautifully drawn until the rigged conclusion.

There is no such cold character in *Aristocrats,* which seems Friel's most Chekhovian job of character drawing. Possibly in Casimir there is a startlingly successful attempt to humanise a Dickensian grotesque. I may possibly be being seduced by John Kavanagh's memorable playing of the part, but I suspect that Friel is having here the best of both worlds, of exaggeration and realism.

Francis Hardy, the main character of *Faith Healer,* is probably Friel's most arresting cold creation since Fox. Both men are something of a mountebank, and their wives and friends do not really understand their urge to self-destruction. Neither perhaps do their audiences, but if Hardy is nearly as enigmatic as Fox, his play is considerably more interesting.

In *Faith Healer,* Friel attempts one of the most difficult of all dramatic tasks, the unfolding of a story entirely by monologues. There is little in the writing of the four monologues that is hugely eloquent or witty, but there is an abundance to act. Shaw once said, without total truth, that he conceived of his function as being mainly the creation of parts for actors. Although *Faith Healer* quickly failed in New York and was not very successful in London, it is a solid and meaty acting play. Although it substitutes narration for a dramatised story, the absorbing characterization fully makes up for the loss.

Translations, however, has been more successful, and the reason doubtless is that it conventionally presents rather than describes its story. A comment like Irving Wardle's 'I have never been more certain of witnessing the première of a national classic',[4] is typical of the praise heaped upon the play. The striking technical innovation of the play is the split-language device, which is as effective and more original than the split-personality of *Philadelphia, Here I Come!* There is a sprinkling of Greek and Latin classical tags in the play, but the main languages are meant to be English and Irish. Friel's innovation consists in having the Irish also spoken as English. The audience thus understands everything, while an onstage character nominally speaking Irish will not be understood by any of the English speaking characters. This device allows intriguing possibilities for irony and, particularly in the love scene between the English-speaking man and the Irish-speaking girl, for comic pathos.[5] In a general sense, the language device also underlines the broad theme of the play, about the gulf between cultures. However, one of the characters is a mute who is being taught to talk, but who relapses into silence when she realises her teacher loves someone else. So Friel may also more broadly be saying that the failure of language is a symptom of the failure of sympathy.

This technical device is so striking that it may have blinded some critics to a number of telling flaws in the play. The most arresting character, the hedge schoolmaster, is not the main character, and has little to do with the plot. The three young men who impel the plot are not really memorable. Also, some crucial developments of the plot occur between scenes, and the conclusion of the plot is really only implied.[6] Once the theatrical novelty of the split-language has worn off, the play's conventional faults may make it seem less dazzling than it did in its initial performances.

To unIrish audiences, the play had a second novelty of being an historical piece about a generally unfamiliar time and place. Irish theatregoers, however, may be reminded strongly of Michael J. Molloy to whom the play seems to owe a good deal. The rural past in *The King of Friday's Men* and many other plays has been distinctly Molloy's province in recent years; and, when Friel enters it, he seems to borrow certain of Molloy's characters, particularly the Man of Learning in *The Visiting House* and Sadie the mute girl in *The Wood of the Whispering*.

Friel is not interesting because he is enormously innovative. His experiments may seem sometimes very fresh or sometimes rather stale, but in either instance they are really variations of previous work. I doubt that it is possible to be truly theatrically innovative any more, and there is nothing wrong in standing on the shoulders of O'Neill or Brecht, or of Chekhov or Molloy. Indeed, in Friel's case there is a good deal that is right, for his more striking technical features have become the most effective palliative for his ferocious themes. Shaw used comedy to sugarcoat the pill of didacticism. Friel's main thematic pre-occupations seem a loneliness and a personal isolation that are suicidally powerful − suicidal at least for success in the commercial theatre. With such cold characters as his Fox and his Frank Butler and his Francis Hardy, his plays really need, and often get, an extraordinary technical camouflage. If they were less fascinatingly told, I doubt that audiences would accept them. Friel's characters are not Misanthropes and Gullivers; they are too beaten, too beyond disillusionment's anger. They may not be entirely humanly plausible or explicable, but their stories are sometimes told so arrestingly that they seem so.

V

Since 1967, Hugh Leonard has continued to write prolifically for television and films as well as for the theatre, and he is probably the biggest money-maker of any current Irish playwright. The New York success of *Da* in 1978 made his name as well known as Brian Friel's, and as respected. In 1980, the Off-Broadway production of *Summer* and the Broadway production of *A Life* did not critically or commercially repeat the success of *Da,* but they did solidify his good reputation.

Leonard's most recent stage work has been his original stories which verge on tragi-comedy, but well into the seventies he continued to write occasional adaptations. His work with late nineteenth century French farce, such as Labiche's *Célimare,* or with modern comic-farce, such as Waterhouse's *Billy Liar,* further honed his already formidable technical facility. A farce by Labiche or Feydeau has an inordinately complicated structure, demanding a breakneck running in and out of doors, misunderstandings and mistaken identies, and plot complications galore. In such a vehement complexity, there is little room for character drawing and none for theme or humanity. Such a play is an intricate, smoothly functioning machine for producing laughter. A Shaw would have loathed it, but there is no gainsaying its technical difficulty; and Leonard was not long in producing a modern Irish version of the form in his hectic farce, *The Patrick Pearse Motel.* That play is simply entertainment, but an entertainment that few of Leonard's Irish contemporaries would have the expertise to produce.

Leonard has always basically been a comic writer, but he has not confined himself to one particular area of comedy. The weekly newspaper columns which he has written since his return to Ireland ten years ago are generally satirical in intent and often witty in their phrasing. Indeed, as farce perfected his ability to structure a play, journalism has given him practice in how to structure a quip, a gag, a pun or a mot. He can fashion as deft a laugh line as Neil Simon, and he can fashion dozens of them.

These remarks may suggest that I think there is a formula for the structuring of farce as well as for the structuring of a laugh line. Actually, there are probably six or eight most usual ways to structure a laugh line. A journeyman writer such as, say, George Kaufman was generally successful but mechanical; and his plots and dialogue (if not always his characterisation) were more jerrybuilt than inspired. One can, however, take the formula for farce and the tricks of comic dialogue, and with luck and inspiration transcend the formulas and the tricks. The great example is probably Wilde's *The Importance of Being Earnest.* The difference between *Earnest* and either Kaufman's *Merrily We Roll Along* or Leonard's *Patrick Pearse Motel* is the difference between an individual and a conventional imagination.

Leonard, who has tried a good deal more than Kaufman or Jean Kerr or Neil Simon or Alan Ayckbourn, has sometimes turned to the most imaginative area of comedy — fantasy. In fantasy, if the quality of imagination is poor, the play is poor; and in fantasy Leonard has so far been at his weakest. His *Au Pair Man* of 1966 was a satirical allegory about the relations between England and Ireland. Satire deals, however, with what is wrong with reality, and pure fantasy deals with what is right with unreality; and Leonard was stronger in this play when his feet were more on the ground, than elsewhere when his head was in the clouds. He had already tried an adaptation of a much purer fantasy, his *When the Saints Go Cycling In* (1965) which was a version of Flann O'Brien's *The Dalkey Archive*. In recent years he has written one original fantasy, *Time Was,* produced by the Abbey in 1976. And he had even flirted with fantasy as early as 1958 in his charming farce *Madigan's Lock*. However, fantasy is a quality that cannot be learned. You can learn the form of farce or the form of a gag by insight and imagination. But fantasy is particularly original imagination, and the quality of imagination in *Time Was* was too bland to be redeemed even by Leonard's always facile dialogue. The basic idea of the play is that characters from the movies come alive and disastrously erupt into real life. Obviously, there are superb possibilities here, particularly for an old-movie buff like Leonard. They were possibilities only thinly realised, though, and little developed.

Incidentally, the final gag of the play was the appearance of Laurel and Hardy. Nothing was done with them; they just appeared as a topper. It was as if, having thought of the gag, Leonard's creative imagination clicked off. When, however, he does not have to imagine, but can simply initate a form or emulate an idea, he can be brilliant. A half-hour television comedy utilising the Laurel and Hardy figures is one of the funniest short things that he has written.

However, Leonard's growing reputation has not been based on imitation, but on original work — chiefly, the plays *Da, Summer* and *A Life*. All of them have beautifully wrought lines, and there are one or two delicious comic situations. But, although their mode is mainly comic, they are ultimately serious plays which intend to move their audiences. This ultimate seriousness has always existed in the best comic writers — Aristophanes, Voltaire, Mark Twain, Shaw — and there was seriousness in Leonard from almost the beginning, from his second play, *A Leap in the Dark* of 1957. Until recently, his purely comic work, whether original or emulative, has rightly overshadowed his serious work such as *The Poker Session* or *Mick and Mick*. Since *Da,* however, the tools that he honed in his long period of journeyman playwriting have been used to fashion his most significant and most admired work.

Of these late plays, *Da* is the most significant and the best known. The title character is unquestionably one of the richest creations of recent Irish drama. Da is a simple figure of a self-less man. He is drawn with no great psychological complexity, but there was no great psychological complexity in Captain Boyle either. If Da is a one-joke character, so also is the immortal Wilkins Micawber. What redeems the simplicity and distinguishes the character is the great warmth with which he is viewed. He is quite the most sympathetically drawn of all the dozens of characters that Leonard has created, and so far about the only one that will be remembered.

Warmth and human sympathy are not Leonard's strong points as a writer. Even in this touching, moving play, warmth is not omnipresent. Da is not the main character, for instance; his foster-son, Charlie, is. But although Charlie is in the centre of the plot and gets all of the funny lines and even clearly bears much resemblance to Leonard himself, one does not really give a damn about him. He is neither warm, nor memorable, nor very interesting.

If one feels a cold disinterest in Charlie, that quality of coldness is what debilitates most of Leonard's original work. A minor character in *Da* is Drumm, and one wonders why, except as a contrast to Da, such a stiff, sour, unlovable character is in the play. He is there, of course, because he interests Leonard, and he interests Leonard so much that he is made the main character of *A Life*.

There are certainly cold, self-absorbed people in life, and the artist has usually ignored them or relegated them to minor roles. In Irish drama, the eminent example of such a character is Paul Vincent Carroll's unforgettable Canon Skerritt of *Shadow and Substance*. Judged by such high standards, Drumm rather pales. However, his sardonic cast is aided by many witty, caustic lines, and he is firmly established as a most definite character. When, however, Skerritt is pushed at the end of *Shadow and Substance* to rebel against his character, the audience is convinced. When Drumm at the end of *A Life* turns for the first time sympathetically to his shadowy wife, he is unbelievable, and we have merely an unconvincing upbeat twist to end the play.

Through 95% of the play, Drumm – this cold, abrasive, unlovable man – exists. He is fully created, memorable, and even succeeds in making the audience care for him. The attempt to draw such a character is admirable, courageous and, until the ending, most successful.

The other characters are not really created. The antagonist, the girl whom Drumm did not marry, is necessarily given a lot of space, but she never quite comes alive. In her husband, Leonard attempts only a caricature, but it is a fine caricature and his comedy is a necessity to the second act. Drumm's wife is a completely unconvincing stock figure whom Leonard spends little time on, and who therefore hurts the play.

One American reviewer commented that the long flashback scenes to the characters' youth add nothing to the plot. I think they do; indeed, a central part of the plot, Drumm's losing the girl, occurs in the flashbacks. And also a central part of the theme requires flashbacks; and that is that a person is what he is over a long time, and that long time does not so much develop him as solidify him. Drumm's final about-face denies this theme, but denies it unconvincingly. Still, the American reviewer was right in one thing: plot in Leonard's original work is of less importance, and a good deal weaker, than it was in his adaptations and entertainments. The reason, of course, is not that Leonard cannot handle plot; he has often demonstrated that he can handle it consummately. He is simply interested in other things, and one fine quality of his original work is that he makes us more interested in them than in plot.

In his serious original work, Leonard is a very personal playwright. One feels that Friel's characters have a broader social base, and that Leonard's exist only on a plane of personal relations. There is an authorial narcissism here which is awfully hard to overcome in the public emotional forum of the theatre. It is a considerable testimony to Leonard's growing powers that he has occasionally overcome it.[7]

VI

After Friel and Leonard, the most highly regarded playwrights of the last decade or so have been Thomas Murphy, Thomas Kilroy and Eugene McCabe.

Through my sheer ignorance, Murphy was not mentioned in *After the Irish Renaissance,* but he certainly should have been because of the Joan Littlewood production of *A Whistle in the Dark* in London in 1961. At the time, Kenneth Tynan described Murphy's account of the Irish in England as 'the most uninhibited display of brutality that the London theatre has ever witnessed.' Since then, Edward Bond and others have considerably surpassed Murphy for brutality, but the savage impact of this play remains.

Murphy was born in Tuam, County Galway in 1935. He taught for several years at Mountbellew Vocational School, becoming at the same time involved in amateur dramatics and working on plays of his own. In particular, he collaborated with a friend, Noel O'Donoghue, on an effective one-act about a rural dance, entitled *On the Outside.*

After the Littlewood production of *Whistle in the Dark,* he turned to writing full-time and lived in London until 1970. He then moved back to Ireland, and had several well-received plays produced at the Abbey. In 1972, the Irish Academy of Letters voted him an award for distinction in literature, and in 1973 he was appointed to the

Abbey Theatre's Board of Directors. His new plays are usually staged at the Abbey, and, despite a recent year's sabbatical from writing, they appear with regularity. Lately he has occasionally turned his hand to directing.

As with Friel, it is impossible to predict what a new Murphy play will be like, and this eclecticism is one of his most interesting characteristics. Unlike Friel, however, Murphy's plays have a considerable unevenness. They can be very good, or they can seem to be very good.

Probably Murphy's best work is the play which was first published as *The Fooleen* and then produced at the Abbey in 1969 with the more ungainly title of *A Crucial Week in the Life of a Grocer's Assistant*. This is a play with obvious similarities in technique and content to Friel's *Philadelphia*. It is the story of an imaginative young man frustrated by life in a rural village and indulging in dramatised daydreams. Although not as accomplished a play as Friel's, *The Crucial Week* has more warmth than most of Murphy's work; and the writing, while mainly simple and straightforward, has moments which are something more. For instance, Miko's speech in Scene Eleven:

I let you down? Well, bejingoes! Well, bejaney-mack-tonight! Well, you're a nice one anyway! Did you come to collect it at the appointed time and place? And I snook it out of the store on Wednesday morning. And haven't I compromised myself forevermore with Mary in Gavins' pub asking her to conceal it till you collected it! What will she be looking for off me in return! Won't I have to give her my all! Tee-hee-hee. And it was lying there in Gavins' all day Wednesday, and all day Thursday and all day yesterday. Be-the-hokies, when I called in for a quick one this morning and learned it was still there! What if it was uncovered by someone? What if my boss was in having a quiet creme de menthe with Michael T. Gavin, chatting understandable hatred of cock-roaches, sees one scuttling under the bottom shelf. He bends with his mallet poised and − 'Hello! What's that nice little portmanteau doing there, Mary?' 'A portmanteau?' says my boss, interjecting, having an understandable interest in suitcases. What? Sure, I could have been arrested, in chains! Bejaney-mack-tonight, I said to myself, get it out of here lively; you'll get no satisfaction from John Joe Moran! And I snook it back to its own little nest in the store.[8]

This fine speech is a little stage-Irish, and far from Molloy or even Keane, but it does have a theatrical vitality to it.

Much of the rest of Murphy strikes me as either pedestrian or pretentious. *Famine,* produced at the Abbey in 1968, is a serious attempt to deal in a big way with the great national trauma of

the nineteenth century. There are passages in it that strive toward
eloquence, and none more effectively than this long speech of Dan
in Scene Eleven:

Whisht now a minute and riddle me this. Bhi fear is fear is fear. . . Hah?
Yis, sure I seen O'Connell once. Yis, yis, yis. The Liberator — didn't we,
Brian? We did. And we waved. And he waved. And he smiled. On top of
his horse. The lovely curly head on him. He did, did, waved with his
hat. . . Aaaa, but the day we got our freedom! Emancy-mancy — what's
that, Nancy? — Freedom, boys! Twenty-nine was the year, and it didn't
take us long putting up the new church. The bonfires lit, and cheering with
his reverence, Father Daly, yis. And I gave Delia Hogan the beck behind
his back. I had the drop in and the urge on me. [*Laughs.*] Oh! — Oh!
— Oh! that's alright, said Delia, winking, but the grass is wet. . . .[9]

The speech goes on for much longer, and obviously offers an
opportunity, if not for eloquence, at least for a vigorous, characteris-
ing reading. Still, the speech does remind us of similar and more
effective ones by Michael Molloy, particularly his great codas in *The
Wood of the Whispering* and *The Visiting House*. In sum, *Famine*
is an earnest play but not one which rises to its theme. O'Flaherty
did it much more memorably in his novel of the same name, and
Cecil Woodham-Smith did it more strikingly in her non-fictional *The
Great Hunger*.

Murphy's other major plays strike me as having an intellectual
coldness about them, as well as a thematic portentousness and a
distinct feebleness of plot. These other major plays would probably
be *The Orphans, The Morning after Optimism* and *The Sanctuary
Lamp*. *The Orphans* first appeared as a staged reading by the now-
defunct Play Circle in, I think, early 1968, and I was very happy
to publish it in 1974. The play is a rather cold tragi-melodrama of
a family, and I do not think that anyone connected with it has felt
more than respect and interest, for it is not a piece to call forth
enthusiasm or to generate warmth. Nor are Murphy's *The Morning
after Optimism* and *The Sanctuary Lamp,* although the semi-allegory
of the first and the religious implications of the second have tended
to impress. I think that both pieces, which certainly had some
Abbey success, were probably more respected than enjoyed. The fantasy of the first is not very fantastic, and the situation in the second
is stronger than the plot or the characterization. Both plays have
some merits and are obviously highly serious, but neither to my mind
makes its seriousness clear or strong. There are nice small touches,
nice satiric points, but little story telling or little fineness of dialogue.
In both the intention is more impressive than the vague execution.

There are a handful of small pieces, however, which show Murphy somewhat less pretentiously. *The White House,* produced by the Abbey in 1972, is really two one-act pieces which both occur in the same public house. One, about the publican who fancies he resembles John F. Kennedy, has a rather silly premise; but the other about young people regarding their youth in a country town has some of the strength of *A Crucial Week.* So also does the one-act *On the Inside,* produced at the Project in 1974 as a companionpiece to the 1959 collaboration *On the Outside.* I have not seen *The Vicar of Wakefield* adaptation, which Murphy did in 1974 for the Abbey, but some perceptive people tell me that it was warm and adroit.

The J. Arthur Maginnis Story was done by the Irish Theatre Company at the Pavilion in Dun Laoghaire in 1977. It was a perhaps satirical farce which a talented cast and lively direction could not save. The script seemed a jocular banality startling from an interesting writer of some proven strength.

After *Maginnis,* Murphy took a sabbatical from playwriting, and his subsequent work I have not seen. It included, however, a one-act about the death of J. M. Synge, a play called *The Blue Macushla* which attempted apparently without great success to tell a contemporary story in terms of old gangster movies, and an adaptation of *The Informer* which was produced in the 1981 Theatre Festival.

Murphy's work so far is a most mixed bag. His best things are the reveries about his youth in the West; his most admired things, *The Morning After Optimism* and *The Sanctuary Lamp,* seem to me more portentous than important. How he will continue to develop is anybody's guess.

Thomas Kilroy has been an academic, a critic and a prize-winning novelist as well as a playwright. He received an M. A. from University College, Dublin, and has lectured there and at several American universities, and is currently a professor of English at University College, Galway. After various fugitive criticisms of considerable perception, he really first made his mark in 1971 as the author of *The Big Chapel,* a low-keyed but quite satisfying historical novel. His first and best stage play, *The Life and Resurrection of Mr. Roche,* had been presented two years earlier by the Abbey. This is a strong, well-characterised study of middle-aged bachelor clerks in Dublin. His *The O'Neill,* which was presented at the Peacock also in 1969, is an historical play whose plain prose seems inadequate for the scope and intended grandeur of its subject. *Tea and Sex and Shakespeare,* presented by the Abbey in 1976, is a contemporary play about a dreaming young writer, but lacks sufficient plot to sustain it for two acts. *Talbot's Box,* which was first presented at the Peacock in October, 1977, was then moved upstairs to the Abbey stage, and had also a short run in London. This two-act is a study of the Dublin worker saint or masochist Matt Talbot. To me, the Talbot of the play seemed neither clearly nor memorably drawn, and the dialogue had only lucidity when it needed eloquence. For instance, this speech of Talbot toward the end:

TALBOT [*Flinging out his arms.*] Get thee behind me, Satan. [*Pauses, gasping, then quietly.*] They said: Lave him alone. Sure it's only Matt. Sure what'd he know about anything? Sure he's not in this world at all. [*Memory.*] 'N all those years I seen the world made right and straight in me own room. Was it dreaming I was? With them terrible things still going on the streets. Oh, Gawd, will it ever change in this world? [*Cry.*] Christ let out! Haven't I been yer auld fool long enough? [*Change.*] God forgive me! It's afraid o' the last darkness I am. When I should see it as the start of Eternal Light. There is a little distance left to me to go. [*Gesturing back to the other figures.*] Leave me to go it alone! Leave me![10]

If this is to be an eloquent moment in the theatre, the actor will have to find his own way. These words point in the right direction, but they do not chart the course.

In 1981, Kilroy effectively transposed Chekhov's *Seagull* to the West of Ireland. Obviously he has not yet congealed into a style or a subject, and it is impossible to predict what his next play might be like or about. All of his work has points of interest, but to date his finest achievement is his novel.

Eugene McCabe was born in Glasgow in 1930, was educated at University College, Cork, and was for ten years or so a dairy farmer in Monaghan before he turned full-time to writing. He has published both fiction and plays, and often does both a dramatic and a fictional version of the same story. He first came to notice with his 1964 play, *The King of the Castle,* which won the first Irish Life Drama Award and was strongly championed by the *Irish Times* critic, Seamus Kelly. The piece is a well-observed realistic rural drama about the triangle of an older man, his young wife and a young man. This situation will recall many other plays, such as T. C. Murray's *Autumn Fire,* Sidney Howard's *They Knew What They Wanted* and Eugene O'Neill's *Desire Under the Elms.* In fact, if one were tracing ancestry, one could go back as far as Euripides and Sophocles. I am not suggesting influence or imitativeness, but really that McCabe latched on to one of the central stories of Western culture. That fact gives much strength to the play. The prototypical story, combined with the author's good ear and sound working out of the plot, made the play in production seem even better than its more than adequate merits. *The King of the Castle* is no masterpiece, but it is sound, moving theatre.

Neither *Breakdown* of 1966 nor *Swift* of 1969 has been published. I have not seen *Breakdown,* but I saw the Tyrone Guthrie Abbey production of *Swift* twice. Despite Mac Liammóir in his last ambitious role, the play seemed rambling and hardly as savage as its subject; nevertheless, it was a better retelling than the versions of Longford or Carroll.

In 1970, McCabe wrote a trilogy of plays for television about the current Northern troubles. These pieces received an elaborate production by RTE, and were much admired. I thought them myself a bit simplistic even for television, particularly the segment called *Victims,* which was also issued separately as a short novel. Another television treatment of the North, *Cancer,* also appeared as a short story, and contains an effective parallel of a particular story to the general political situation. The television play, *Roma,* was likewise a short story; and its quality − and McCabe's quality generally − may be suggested by the following randomly selected exchange of dialogue:

MARIA. You do.
BENNY. I try.
MARIA. And what's to be done?
BENNY. Prayer and penance and . . . .
  [*Long Pause.*]
MARIA. You pray a lot Benny?
BENNY. I try.
  [*Benny shakes his head. Long pause.*]
BENNY. All the bad places should be shut.
MARIA. Yes?
BENNY. Pubs, dance halls, all like that.
MARIA. Everywhere?
BENNY. Yes.
MARIA. How?
BENNY. I don't know.
MARIA. Ever hear of prohibition Benny?
BENNY. No.
MARIA. When did you leave school?
BENNY. I was twelve.
  [*Maria nods.*][11]

Actors can make this passage play, for it is exact enough, but it is not really interesting as dialogue. It is somewhat terser than McCabe always is, but it suggests that he writes with a realistic flatness. By the quality of his writing, then, I think one is justified in saying that McCabe is not going to rise to eloquence. Indeed, much of his work has a simple crudity, and the texture of it is generally journeyman stuff. As one perhaps slightly pedantic symptom, he has never learned, or at least does not bother to use, conventional punctuation. (This is not merely pedantic. Directors and actors, no matter how good, need all the directions, all the nuances and nice distinctions that they can get; and punctuation is invaluable for precision and subtlety.)

What is most effective about McCabe is that he chooses strong contemporary situations, and treats them with understanding and compassion. Indeed, his content and his ability to arrange it into an effective story often elevate his work into some of the more powerful being written. That is quite enough to compel attention and interest for the moment. The moment quickly passes, however, and, unless McCabe adds refinement of technique to his obvious strengths, he will be gone with it.

Several Northern writers other than McCabe — and, in one notable play, Friel — have dealt with the Northern problem. The soundest and most satisfying treatment has been by the oldest writer, John Boyd, who was born in 1912. His *The Assassin* (1969), *The Flats* (1971), *The Farm* (1972) and *Guests* (1974) are a substantial body of craftsmanlike work. The last three plays were presented by the Lyric Players Theatre with whom Boyd is connected, but his work has been so recently published that I have just not assimilated it yet.

Although he was born in Cork, the poet and playwright Patrick Galvin has also been connected with the Lyric as a writer in residence, and the theatre has produced and published three of his plays. The most striking is *We Do It for Love,* a ballad opera whose tunes do not compensate for the thinness of the script.

An equally thin Northern writer is Stewart Parker, who was born in Belfast in 1941, and educated at Queen's University where he was one of the group of poets centering around Philip Hobsbaum. His play *Spokesong* is a musical which was produced to considerable acclaim in London in 1976, and which sees Northern life from the vantage point, over the years, of a bicycle shop. The London production must have been superb, and the Long Wharf production in America good, for the play to have been so admired. For the production by the Irish Theatre Company in Dun Laoghaire was so lame that the poverty of the script was all too apparent. The tunes were imitative pop ballads by a Northern song writer who had once written 'Red Sails in the Sunset' and 'South of the Border'; and both tunes and book really need a substantial lift from the actors and the director if this play is going to come alive. A later play, *Catchpenny Twist,* is about pop singers and the Northern troubles, and strikes me as a bit less thin but very far-fetched. The still later *Nightshade* is about magic and morticians, and is both mystifying and deadly.

John Wilson Haire had his *Within Two Shadows* produced at the Lyric in 1972, and his *Bloom of the Diamond Stone* produced at the Abbey in 1973, and has since had some success in London. However, he seems as thin as the other writers, and with his Montague and Capulet love story in *Bloom* he inevitably recalls St. John Ervine's treatment of the situation in *Mixed Marriage* of sixty years earlier.

Ron Hutchinson was born in Lisburn and raised in Belfast until his family moved to England in his early teens. His first produced play was the 1977 *Says I, Says He,* which received the George Devine award in London, and was successfully staged by the Phoenix in New York in 1979. This is a Behan-like study of chicanery in the building trade which uses the Northern troubles more as background than as central theme. Like Parker's and Galvin's plays, *Says I, Says He* depends strongly on a theatrical staging, but in characterization and dialogue it gives actors more to play with. Hutchinson has had three later plays produced in London and Dublin, and has done considerable television writing.

J. Graham Reid was born in Belfast and teaches in County Down. His two-act, *The Death of Humpty Dumpty,* was produced by the Peacock in September, 1979, and is one of the most talented of recent debuts. The piece tells of an amiable man who is physically paralyzed in a typical bit of Northern violence, and how his paralysis warps and dehumanizes him. Despite an overly melodramatic ending, the psychological situation is telling, and the hospital milieu is quite believably evoked. His later piece, *A Closed Door*, is less striking, but he remains a writer to watch.

Perhaps just for the record Benedict Kiely's *Proxopera* should be mentioned. This novella was dramatized by Peter Luke and disastrously staged by the Gate in 1978.

Obviously the traumas of the North are finally getting attention from the dramatists, but nothing in any way comparable to O'Casey's sixty-year-old trilogy about the traumas of the South has as yet appeared.

VII

Of the writers who were middle-aged in 1967, Michael J. Molloy has most consistently worked at his trade. However, much of this new work remains unpublished and unproduced, and most of it is not of the calibre of *The King of Friday's Men, The Wood of the Whispering, The Visiting house* or that small masterpiece, *The Paddy Pedlar.* There is one exception, *Petticoat Loose,* produced at the Abbey in 1979. This historical piece describes the effect of folk superstition upon rural lives; and, if it has Molloy's usual faults, it also exhibits his qualities at their strongest. The faults are that the plotting is too convoluted and the play is too long. The qualities are the richness of the dialogue, the bizarre situations and a greater interest in sexuality than has appeared in his previous work. The Abbey production by Tomás Mac Anna was elaborate, but I thought fussy as well as badly miscast in a couple of important roles. In some ways, the production more camouflaged than presented the play's merits. However, the script was Molloy's best in years, and quite comparable to his almost best long plays.

In 1967, John O'Donovan did for the new Abbey a minor piece, called *Dearly Beloved Roger.* Since then, unfortunately, no new work of his has appeared. He has done excellent service for the drama in organising the Society of Irish Playwrights, but his retirement as a playwright seems one of the lamentable wastes of recent years.

Bryan MacMahon has done considerable writing since 1967, but no major work, I think, since the novelization of *The Honey Spike* in that same year. He has written a few short plays of interest, and two of them − *The Death of Biddy Early* and *Jack Furey* − were published in *The Journal of Irish Literature* in 1972. He has also recently allowed a new full-length play, *The Master,* to be produced by amateurs. This is a piece about the long career of a rural teacher, and seems really still a work in progress.

The younger Listowel playwright, John B. Keane, has somewhat broadened his subject matter, but his critical reputation has not grown. His early plays, particularly *Sive* and *Sharon's Grave,* earned him a deserved reputation as a latter-day folk dramatist, a ferocious Kerry version of Michael Molloy. His later plays in the 1960s, such as *The Year of the Hiker* and the impressive *The Field,* seemed successful attempts to portray a waning folk culture in conflict with a modern Ireland. The best of his plays of the 1970s, such as *Big Maggie* and *The Change in Mame Fadden* and *The Good Thing* and *The Chastitute,* seem explorations of attitudes toward sex in modern Ireland. They describe the effects of menopause, of sexual boredom and of sexual frustration; and they have a directness and an absence of portentousness which one did not find in much other work of the decade. Keane remains a box-office draw, and he remains as productive as Friel or Leonard or Murphy, but they are generally considered as much more serious dramatists than he.

There are several reasons for this fact, some persuasive and some unfair. Foremost among the unfair ones is that Keane, unlike Friel or Leonard, has never had a notable commercial success outside of Ireland. In London and particularly in America, Friel and Leonard have both had important runs and critical acclaim; Keane has never had a play in the West End or on Broadway or even Off-Broadway — although at this writing there is talk of an important production of *Big Maggie* for the 1982-83 season in New York. Second among the somewhat unfair reasons is that Keane has been so prolific in his non-dramatic work, and that so much of it has been ephemeral or minor. He has, fairly or not, come to be regarded as a casual entertainer as was once John D. Sheridan and is now Sam McAughtrey. In the 1970s, Keane wrote much for newspapers, and he published a long series of short, epistolary novels about the Irish countryside, as well as several collections of stories and of essays mainly compiled from his newspaper pieces. Some of this material was ripely entertaining, and his *Letters of an Irish T. D.* and its sequel, *Letters of an Irish Minister of State,* are among the funniest Irish books of the decade. Much of his other writing, however, was pretty bland and did nothing to foster the notion that here was a major talent.

And that fact brings up what is probably going to be the critical cliché about Keane: he writes too much and with too little consideration. Most dramatic criticism, including probably a good deal in this volume is simply a rephrasal of such clichés as: Shaw is all head and no heart; O'Neill had all of the requisites for a writer of great tragedy except the ability to write; O'Casey, when he left Ireland in 1926, left his talent behind on the North Circular Road, etc., etc. And I totally regret promulgating a cliché about Keane which ignores what is most important about the man, his quite individual genius. However:

In *The Change in Mame Fadden, The Good Thing* and *The Chastitute,* Keane discusses central problems of modern life with candour and vigour. But at a certain point, he temporises, he fudges, he does not work hard enough, and he usually settles for the entertaining laugh.

Take *The Chastitute.* The hero is a middle-aged, virginal farmer who is frantic for a woman but who, through his conditioning and a series of contrived staged accidents, fails to find one; so at the end, he is glumly, grimly resigned to living and dying a virginal bachelor. This play strikes me, first of all, as an anachronism. The audience laughs at a man of the 1950s, whose problems seem a

bit unbelievable in the 1980s. The fun – and there are some tellingly
funny scenes – is rooted in our memory of puritanism rather than
relevant to our present experience. And, worse, so much is sacrificed to laughs that it is impossible to modulate, as Keane tries, into
a serious statement at the end; and the play remains a collection of
jokes rather than a serious analysis of life.

Take *The Good Thing*. The characters are affluent provincials who
have been married for ten years, and who have enough money to
spend a weekend in Dublin in a hotel like the Burlington. The tasteless
and expensive modernism of the place is an apt symbol for the milieu
that forms the modern Irishman. And the modern Irishman is not
Tom Riordon of James Douglas' television show, which subsequent
writers, like Wesley Burrowes, embalmed into a nostalgic memory.
He is closer to the man with a Mercedes for himself and a Datsun
for his wife. This man and his wife Keane has seen and sensed, and
not caught. Instead, he has dribbled away honest observation in in-
dulgent romance, easy theatricalism, cheap jokes and clichéd writing.
And yet what a fine subject he had.

Take the minor plays: *The Crazy Wall, The Buds of Ballybunnion,* the three one-acts published as *Values.* All of these are so quick,
so thin and so ill-considered that they trivialise and debase one of
the few individual talents that the Irish drama has seen since O'Casey
or Behan.

Reading over these past few pages, it seems to me that I have been
harsher on Keane than on many other writers discussed in this book.
The reason, of course, is that his best work arouses such high
expectations.

Several other middle-aged men have made their mark in the last
dozen years, particularly three members of the Council of the Society
of Irish Playwrights – Michael Judge, David Hayes and Liam Mac
Uistin. Each, despite a number of productions, has so far published
only one long and one or two short plays. Michael Judge is a Dublin
schoolmaster, born in 1921, and his published play is *Saturday Night
Women* which was produced in 1971. This is a satirical Woman's
Lib play with an extraordinarily funny prologue that unfortunately
upstages much of the flatter stuff that follows. Judge has had short
and long plays at the Abbey, the Peacock, the Project, the Eblana
and in the 1980 Theatre Festival. He has also done some television
and much radio work. In fact, he has done entirely too much radio
work, especially on the serial *Harbour Hotel.* This constant bread
and butter work has consumed enough time for him to have written
several major pieces for the theatre. Judge has a fine comic in-
telligence and a command of his craft; and, as he already has enough

bread, plus a few dollops of jam, it is time to put his talents to serious rather than hack work, though it looks as if the serious work will be a novel.

David Hayes was born in 1919 and worked in industry for many years before turning fulltime to writing. He is currently employed as a script consultant for RTE. His stage work and his radio work have both won prizes. His one published full-length play is *Sorry! No Hard Feelings?,* a sardonic realistic fantasy about the growth of Fascism in the state.

Liam Mac Uistin writes both in Irish and English, and his only published play to date, *Post Mortem,* was originally performed in an Irish version at the Peacock in March 1971. This is a short two-act, set in a Gaeltacht village in the west. It truly evokes this dying culture, and interestingly sees it through the eyes of a dead emigrant brought home to be buried. In its English version, it is a melancholy and often beautifully written piece. Here is a part of one of the speeches by the dead man:

Yes, they're coming at last! Soon they'll be leaving their farms and shops, their white-washed cottages and shiny new bungalows built with Yankee dollars and Dublin grants . . . . They'll be coming soon in their carts and cars along the dungy road to Puckleme, coming to me and my requiem. Come on so! Hurry will ye? Amn't I long enough waiting for ye? [*Pause.*] I wonder what the weather's like out there? It should be raining cats and dogs, today of all days, but I'd say it's not — not with my luck! No, I suppose the sun is splitting the rocks, beaming on every bog, shining on the stone-stitched fences and on the black-bottomed boats now high and dry like beached whales. . . . [12]

Of James Douglas, I find it hard to write, for I know him and his work too well. We have spent much time in the last ten years working on six or eight rarely or never produced plays; and this fact certainly slowed down the production of his own stage work. In part, though, he himself is to blame, for he has spent an inordinate amount of time in radio and television writing which is a good deal more simplistic than his stage plays.

Since 1967, Douglas has produced but one new full-length stage play, *The Savages.* This was given a staged reading by Play Circle early in 1968 at the Peacock, with a fine cast that included Cyril Cusack, Anna Manahan and Aideen O'Kelly. Then in, 1970, it was effectively staged at the Eblana with Eamon Keane, Martin Dempsey and May Cluskey. Its only subsequent revival was in 1980, Off-Off Broadway at the Irish Arts Center. The piece is a telling diagnosis of the second generation of the Irish middle-class businessman, and a perceptive indictment of the erosion of values in a modern, decreasingly Irish world. It has little of the mannered dialogue of his early work, and its prime fault is that it still needs a rigorous cutting, perhaps by as much as twenty-five minutes.

In 1978, *The Painting of Babbi Joe* had its stage premiere Off-Off Broadway. I had a small hand in the writing of this, but basically the play is Douglas's, and a stage adaptation of an effective television play. The faults of the stage play, which is about a triangular love affair between two house painters and a somewhat wilted young woman, stem from the simplicity of the television script and are, without a basic rewriting, unavoidable. The qualities are Douglas's good ear for argot, and a compassion for his characters that one often misses in Friel, Leonard, Murphy, McCabe or Kilroy.

That good ear and that deep, even at times cloying, compassion are evident in two companion one-acts, set in a Dublin pub. One of these, *Time Out of School,* won the O. Z. Whitehead award in one of the Theatre Festivals, and was briefly revived for a lunchtime production at the Peacock in 1978. Both seem to me indulgently sentimental and overlong.

Douglas's short stories, which he possibly enjoys doing more than his plays, have in contrast an often startling sour power and eminently need to be collected.

In 1968, G. P. Gallivan had a production at the Lantern of his modern political play, *A Beginning of Truth,* which remains unpublished but which strikes me as close to his best work. In 1971, a documentary drama, *The Dail Debates,* was presented in the Peacock, but proved little more than an undramatic stringing together of excerpts from the Treaty discussions. In 1977, *Dev* was given at the Project, and was a loose chronicle of some events in de Valera's life rather than an effectively plotted play. In 1980, a commercial 'musical' based on the life of John MacCormack was something of a crowd-pleaser because of the songs which were sung by a popular tenor, but MacCormack's life obdurately resisted drama. In 1981, an earlier play, *Watershed,* was published. This was a rambling, lengthy, three-handed lament about the life of a middle-class couple, and to this reader it lacked structure, interesting characterization and any deftness in dialogue.

A couple of years ago, I wrote:

Obviously, Gallivan's main preoccupation in the theatre has been the subject of Irish politics, but, with an exception of two, his work has been worthy but somewhat lacking in bite. Still, more than any other contemporary Irish playwright he has addressed himself constantly to a significant topic. In his never less than competent plays, he has worked quietly for an adult and untrivial theatre.[13]

While not reneging on Gallivan's usual high seriousness and his intelligent pre-occupation with political drama, I would now add that, after twenty years of professional playwriting, he has not significantly grown. Both *Dev* and *Watershed* are less professional than some of his earlier work. The plotting is botched, the characters are dull, and the writing is without distinction and sometimes even theatre sense. That seems a cruel dismissal, but in this same period Friel and Leonard have grown immensely, and Gallivan, despite his seriousness and his early promise, has only grown worse. This is an enormous shame, for who else in modern Irish drama has so consistently had such sober and needed pre-occupations?

Two other, more or less middle-aged men made their dramatic debuts in this period, Conor Cruise O'Brien and Desmond Forristal. O'Brien, as politician and commentator on politics and literature, is well known outside of Ireland; and that fact must have had much to do with the commercial production of his 1968 play, *Murderous Angels*. The piece is simply much too thoughtful for a Broadway play, as also are the three one-acts collected in *Herod, Reflections on Political Violence* (1978). The plays are more than dramaturgically adequate and they are lucidly written, but they are not strong in those most urgent theatrical elements of character or story.

In his thoughtfulness, Forristal somewhat resembles O'Brien, and his best play, *Black Man's Country* (Gate, 1974), is set in Africa as is much of *Murderous Angels*. Forristal's first play, *The True Story of the Horrid Popish Plot* (Gate, 1972), is an historical play with that rarity on the recent Irish stage, some witty lines. His last work to date, *The Seventh Sin* (Gate, 1976), is also an historical piece but duller than its predecessors. One patron leaving the theatre met a friend and explained, 'What's it about? Oh, it's about a couple of oul' Popes.'

Nevertheless, a flip tone is hardly apt for either *Murderous Angels* or *Black Man's Country*. Both are flawed but quite interesting, adult works. Both Doctor O'Brien and Father Forristal lead busy, involved lives in society, and so their occasional playwriting is done with their left hands. That is unfortunate for the theatre.

VIII

In recent years, Dublin has been particulary receptive to symptoms of young talent. The Arts Council's grant has grown, and the Council has been optimistic about and generous toward the young. Indeed, the tolerance extended toward the young writer has probably resulted in rather fulsome praise and little real criticism of flaws. Hence, there have been laudatory notices for young poets who do not understand poetic form, for young novelists who are baffled by the structure of the normal English sentence, and for young playwrights whose confusion ranges from punctuation to plotting. This may seem a churlish remark, but I can support it by many instances not only from the inexperienced, new writer, but also from the established older one. In an Introduction to a recent volume, a member of the Irish Academy of Letters wrote not only in a slovenly and ambiguous style, but also had three flagrant errors of grammar on just the first page. An admired first volume of stories so consistently misspelled several words that the faults could not have been typos. Most of the interesting plays published by Writers' Co-op and by Turoe Press are nearly unencumbered by punctuation; it is as if the writers heard words well enough, but had small notion of how to convey them onto the page. In future ages, such writers have perhaps a future by disseminating their intentions via tape and cassette. And perhaps in such enlightened times we may also have learned the pretentious inutility of knives and forks and table napkins.

But, of course, I am not talking about inessential decoration; I am talking about the failure to make accurate distinctions. Gross pedantry on my part, no doubt.

Notable among the younger writers is Heno Magee whose first play, *I'm Getting Out of This Kip,* was written in 1968 and produced in 1972. Since then, the Abbey has produced two more of his plays, *Hatchet* in 1972 and *Red Biddy* in 1974. His plays, as James Douglas put it:

. . . explore with bawdy humor, poetic insight, and deep compassion the manners, mores, and morals of Dublin's working-class ghettos. If one treats Behan's theatrical cartoons as a case apart, not since O'Casey have the denizens of the back-streets been put on the stage with such truth and accuracy.[14]

Mary Manning, generally a most acute critic, remarked after a production of *Hatchet* that Magee could be a playwright of brilliance.

Magee was born in Dublin in 1939 of a working-class family. He quit school at fourteen, worked as a messenger boy, then joined the R.A.F., and then returned to Dublin and worked in a tobacco factory. After the success of his plays, he was for several years the drama critic of *The Standard,* and in 1976 he was awarded an Abbey

Theatre bursary and won the Rooney Prize in Literature.

I have not seen or read *I'm Getting Out of This Kip*. However, *Red Biddy* was a long monologue in which a woman explored her past, and in the Peacock production of 1972 its problems seemed to defeat even the talents of Maire Kean. One problem is simply technical, and the same problem as in Yeats's *Words upon the Window Pane:* it is difficult to get an actor to speak in a variety of voices, particularly children's voices.

Hatchet, however, had a fine production, and its two best characters, the mother and the son, were memorably played by May Cluskey and John Kavanagh. Indeed, the playing was so good that the play seemed even better than it is. What it is, basically, is a conventionally told, soundly constructed story of a Dublin working-class area. It is accurately observed; it carries conviction; and it provides a full blueprint for the director and the actors to fill out. That is all it is. To take just one instance, the language. James Douglas says that, 'Magee's characters speak a rich, low-life vernacular. . . . ' I do not think that they do. It is good stage speech, simple, authentic and containing the usual Dublin locutions. Here is a passage taken at random, but I think, nevertheless, a fair sample of the whole:

HATCHET. What's bleedin' goin' on?
BRIDIE. They were arguing.
MRS. B.. I didn't start it.
HATCHET. Shut up, over what?
ANGELA. Your mother threatened to split me.
MRS. B.. That's all, I didn't even touch her.
BRIDIE. It was over the house.
MRS. B.. I just want yis to have it, that's all.
BRIDIE. I told her we didn't want it, and Angela. . . .
MRS. B.. Had to poke her big red nose in, didn't ye?
ANGELA. I have nothing more to say.[15]

This is what the dialogue of the play is like. There is nothing wrong with it, and quite a bit right. It is what the characters would plausibly say, and it allows actors some scope. It is clean, lean, tight, progressive. But it is not rich as O'Casey or Behan or Seamus de Burca even is rich. Of course, O'Casey and Behan were tossing in everything and the kitchen sink, the best of what they had heard while growing up on the north side. What they wrote was much more thickly embroidered than what they heard; in fact, it was so embroidered that it was finally not realistic. O'Casey especially used it as a basis for the creation of his own individual language in the later plays.

So far, Magee is a realist, and so must handle language the way he does. My point, then, is that, while his handling is right and just, it is not rich. And what may be said about the dialogue may be said about the rest of the play. So without going overboard and heralding a new stage genius, one would better say that here is a playwright who has pulled off a fine play and demonstrated competence in his craft. Anything he does in the future will surely be of considerable interest.

Two playwrights who treat somewhat similar material are the Sheridan brothers. They are ten years or so younger than Magee. Jim Sheridan was born in 1949 and Peter Sheridan in 1952. Jim Sheridan has published *Mobile Homes* in 1978 about the social and economic problems of young families living on a caravan site. Peter Sheridan has published *The Liberty Suit* about juvenile prison life in 1978, and also a nineteenth century historical play called *Emigrants* in 1979. Both brothers have good ears for dialogue and some sense of effective theatre, but do not seem to me so far to have created anything strongly warranting revival.

Maeve Binchy made her reputation as a genial, humorous correspondent for *The Irish Times;* indeed, she and Hugh Leonard are probably the most enjoyed newspaper humorists since Myles himself, and that is a hard act to follow. From the late 1970s, Miss Binchy published some fiction and collections of her newspaper columns and wrote several plays for the stage and for television. I know only two of these. Her first piece, *End of Term,* was a one-act done at the Peacock in 1977, and a soundly crafted study of teachers in a girls' school. Her television play, *Deeply Regretted By,* won several awards, and is a moving story of a woman in England whose Irish husband has, unknown to her, another family at home. This piece is underwritten in a terse television style. For instance;

FR. BARRY. Perhaps if I leave you to yourself you won't feel you hate everyone so much.
STELLA. Perhaps.
FR. BARRY. But I have a feeling that this is the time you need me — somebody — Father Flanagan?
STELLA. Not Father Flanagan thank you, not Father anything.
FR. BARRY. Stella what can I do to tell you that there's some kind of friendship some help however watery it may seem. . . .
STELLA. Forget it Father that's the best.
FR. BARRY. Stella.
STELLA. Please don't keep me [?] calling me Stella.
FR. BARRY. Well, I can't keep calling you Mrs. Healy.
STELLA. That's just it. I'm not Mrs Healy am I? I never was.
  [They look at each other for a long time.][16]

Although the proofreading and the punctuation do not help an actor's interpretation, the words seem chosen with much accuracy. And certainly Stella gave that fine actress Joan O'Hara one of her most moving roles.

In an interview in a Philadelphia paper late in 1980 on the occasion of a production of another play, *Half Promised Land,* Miss Binchy came across — perhaps it was the interviewer's fault — as jocularly stage Irish. In her own writings, however, her strongest points are her humour and her warm humanity. With those qualities and with her already demonstrated command of technique, she should write marvellous plays.

Bernard Farrell had his one-act, *Goodbye Smiler, It's Been Nice,* presented at the Lantern in 1975. His *I Do Not Like Thee, Doctor Fell,* was a two-act presented at the Peacock in 1979, and his *Canaries* was one of the most admired pieces in the 1980 Theatre Festival. *Doctor Fell* is a rather dated Black Comedy of Menace about an Encounter Group session. It indicates that Ireland has entered the modern world and that its author has talent, but is not particularly memorable. *Canaries* is a less structured piece about vacationers in the Canary Islands, but has some touches of tolerable satire. *All in Favour Said No,* presented by the Abbey in early 1981, is a broadly satiric piece about a strike. The play starts slowly; it has several characters who are undeveloped comic ideas with nothing to do; and the conclusion with the model train does not strike me as original. However, the second act is quite amusing and has some interesting comic ideas. This satiric farce is Farrell's best work to date, and much better than the mildly pretentious *Dr. Fell* or *Canaries.* All of his work, however, is distinctly modern in its pre-occupations. Farrell looks at the present rather than at the Irish past, and in the present he should certainly find ample material for further light satire.

These are the writers who most interested me in recent years. There are others who might plausibly be discussed — Wesley Burrowes, John Lynch, Kevin Grattan, Lee Gallaher or Joe O'Donnell. Kevin Casey, the sombre but accomplished novelist, has written plays; the clever wordsmith Tom MacIntyre has written plays; Sydney Bernard Smith, the poet, has published an interesting one-act called *Sherca.* And there are still other writers who have been admired, but whose work I do not really like or am not sufficiently familiar with. Perhaps time and greater taste will change all of that. Of this group, however, at least John Arden and his wife Margaretta D'Arcy ought to be noted. The Ardens have lived for some years in the West, and have collaborated on several pieces about Ireland. One is the hugely long *Non-Stop Connolly Show* which took all night to read in

Liberty Hall, and which seems to me thin agit-prop and far from the excellence of Arden's early English work.

It strikes me that many of these judgments may seem harsh. The reason is that this is an interim report between the snap judgment of contemporary journalism and the judicious assessment that comes with the passage of time. Journalistic criticism has a reputation for harshness, and in the days of Shaw or Nathan it sometimes was harsh. However, in those days four or five times as many plays would have been produced in a season, and it was kind to be harsh. To-day, when many fewer plays are produced in any season, critics are much gentler. If only thirty plays are produced on Broadway or in the West End or in Dublin, the critics cannot pan thirty plays. On the contrary, they are going to have to ferret out any shadow of excellence to laud; otherwise, there will be a very scanty season indeed.

So in recent years Dublin critics, like those in New York and London, have greeted rather conventional plays with paeans of praise and bleats of ecstasy. I have even heard one academic critic in Dublin publically declare that the Irish theatre was entering a new renaissance. Was, indeed, in the middle of one. So perhaps this chapter, in reaction against the necessary puffery of the daily press, has been unnecessarily harsh. However, the dust has not yet settled. For some of these writers the battle is not over, and for others it has barely begun. Good plays, even great plays, sometimes take some living with to be fully appreciated. George Fitzmaurice was not widely appreciated until after his death, and only now is Denis Johnston getting his due. Despite some harsh judgments in this chapter, I think that there are a few writers and pieces here that will be played for many years. Despite economics and timidity and sheer bad taste, some interesting plays are somehow being produced and published. It is not exactly a deluge of genius, but it is much more than a trickle of talent.

A FACTUAL APPENDIX

This book is mainly a critical account of playwriting, and not really an historical account of the theatre, but a few facts and dates about the last twelve or fifteen years might not be amiss.

On 18 July 1966, the new Abbey Theatre building was opened for its first performance, and the date was exactly fifteen years from the fire in the old theatre. In the Abbey's fifteen year exile across the river in the Queen's, the artistic quality of the productions and the players and often of the plays considerably declined – not perhaps so considerably as was constantly asserted by critics, but it was not a first-rate company.

Now the company has been in its new house for fifteen years, and its quality has greatly improved. The improvement is quite notable in the set design which is consistently good and often excellent. The costuming and lighting are generally fine. The acting is usually sound, and has often been excellent, and occasionally brilliant. Among the young actors which the Abbey has helped to develop are Donal McCann and John Kavanagh, who are never less than interesting, and who are sometimes superb.[1] However, even those now middle-aged veterans who received their training in the Queen's – no, training is not the word. Even those middle-aged veterans who received their experience in the Queen's have on occasion risen above their range and technique and done memorable work. Of course, there have still been tired performances and stock performances not only by the veterans and the neophytes, but even by the occasional visiting star. This is not the book in which to assess Abbey acting, but it should be stated that the general level is much above that of the Queen's.

Nor is this a place to analyze, as much as an outsider can, the quality of Abbey directing, but I should like to suggest two generalizations. First, the directing also is much beyond the level of the Queen's. The reason is partly that the range of plays presented has been more various and demanding, and partly that the direction has been exposed to and somewhat influenced by outside examples. Second, the directing is, nevertheless, more uneven than any other facet of production. One can see a show on opening night and then see it a week later, and notice how discernably the director's business has oozed away. Or, for example, the London stage can rediscover a piece like O'Keefe's *Wild Oats* and stage it so well that you almost think you are seeing a lost masterpiece; but, when the Abbey gets around to the play a year or two later, the staging will be so pedestrian that the play looks bad.

Nevertheless, the Abbey more than adequately produces the generally important works, or a few works of possible importance, for most of the year; and that fact makes it now the arbiter of Irish theatrical taste. It was not that in the Queen's.

It is not yet apparent how the deaths of Micheál Mac Liammóir in 1978, and of Hilton Edwards in November 1982 will affect the future of the Gate Theatre. Certainly, in the 1970s, with its production of Friel and Forristal and Peter Shaffer, the Gate enjoyed a fine Indian summer. However, Edwards once wrote that the concern of the theatre was always with 'the whole gamut of the stage'. And with its long, varied and distinguished repertoire – that ranged from Aeschylus to Brecht, and from *Hamlet* to *Ten Nights in a Bar Room* – the Gate eminently fulfilled its intention. It gave to the nation examples of expertise and craft; it educated and honed taste; it increased an urbane tolerance and diminished cultural parochialism; it staged masterpieces that inspired terror, and nonsenses that evoked delight. In short, it exemplified a civilised ideal. In short, art. Whether the new members of the Gate board have the theatrical expertise and the dedication to continue a constant and eclectic repertoire into the 1980s is a moot point indeed.

The Irish Theatre Company was formed in 1972, and subsidised by the Irish government for the main purpose of bringing theatre to provincial cities. In its few seasons, the company has had several artistic directors but little consistent policy. It usually produced four plays a year, toured each for six weeks and then brought each into some venue in Dublin for two weeks. Any year's repertoire seems a Gate-like eclecticism that might feature a classic play, a contemporary commercial success, an Irish revival and occasionally a new Irish play. The plays have ranged from a version of Boucicault's *London Assurance,* to a musical about the Beatles, to a couple of new or newish plays by Tom Murphy, Stewart Parker and Tom Kilroy. Few of these choices were exactly venturesome. The Boucicault had been a recent successful revival in London, the Parker and the Kilroy had recently been done in London, and Murphy was one of the most produced Abbey authors. The theatre has not formed a permanent company, and its productions have varied considerably in quality. Its chief problem may be not producing enough to make an impact. And, at the present writing, its funds have been withdrawn, and it is not producing at all.

The little Lantern, after a couple of disasters to its premises in Merrion Square, was finally extinguished. This long-lived group was always an amateur undertaking although one or two of its alumni, like Bosco Hogan, have gone on to professional careers. However, its plays were always approached with high seriousness; and, if it produced no brilliant work, it produced much that was worthy of attention. However uneven its accomplishments, it was always a reminder of high taste, and a conscience. It will be missed.

The same serious approach of the Lantern, and the same serious repertoire, is still somewhat available at another pocket theatre, the Focus, which has something of a bent toward early modern classics, such as Turgenev, Ibsen and Chekhov.

The liveliest and most vivid new theatre is that of the Project Arts Centre which seems to have found a permanent home behind the Olympia. For some years, the group had the inevitable drawbacks of being run by a committee, whose only general area of agreement was that it favoured *avant garde* forms. Those forms had been tested elsewhere first, and nothing really original was forthcoming; but mixed media shows, such as some work by Lee Gallaher, exposed Dublin to a type of theatre it would not otherwise have seen. Most recently, this bent toward theatricalism has been influenced by the Scottish 7:84 Company which uses an open staging, ballad singing and rock music to sugarcoat a social message. The 7:84 Company is not originally inventive, but it performs with great brio. In recent years, the Project has been mainly controlled by the Sheridan brothers whose bent seems firmly theatricalist and socially critical. So far, theory has outstretched technique, and the will has been more impressive than the deeds. But if the theatre is yet, in both its plays and productions, little more than semi-professional, it is also wholly dedicated.

Some of the Project's theatricalism is apparent in another state subsidised group, Siamsa Tire, the National Folk Theatre; and among other regional amateur groups the Druid Theatre of Galway has done some really exciting work, including a production of *The Tinker's Wedding* which was as fine as one could ever expect to see.

II

Also among the facts must come the Obituary, which is a particularly dismal business as a large number of fine writers died. Since the last report, Rutherford Mayne died in 1967, and so did

Walter Macken. Donagh MacDonagh and Seamus Byrne died in 1968, as did Paul Vincent Carroll. St. John Ervine and Kate O'Brien died in 1971. Padraic Colum died in 1972, and the poets Austin Clarke and Padraic Fallon died in 1974, and Maurice Davin-Power not long after. Micheál Mac Liammóir died in 1978, J. Bernard MacCarthy in 1979, and Jack White in 1980. A sad and depressing recital.

Of these writers, Carroll, Ervine, Mayne, MacCarthy and Kate O'Brien had assuredly written all of the plays that they were going to. But who knows about Colum and Mac Liammóir who both produced fine work in their old age? Austin Clarke was writing as well as he ever had, and a couple of plays appeared posthumously. Donagh MacDonagh, Walter Macken, Seamus Byrne and Jack White were not old men.

I am not a great admirer of MacDonagh's verse plays and ballad operas, but their strength is more apparent on the stage than on the page, and I could be wrong. In case I was, I published one of Mac-Donagh's verse plays, *Lady Spider,* a treatment of the Deirdre story, in 1980; and I would point out to the enterprising that there are several other plausible and unpublished MacDonagh scripts.

When he died, Walter Macken still seemed at the height of his very vigorous powers. Although in his last years his interest had really turned away from drama to fiction, he was for a period before his death the artistic director of the Abbey. Also, his last produced play, *The Voices of Doolin,* seemed in its character drawing much subtler stuff than the theatricalities of his early work. Before his death, I was scheduled to see *Doolin* into print, but was not able to − a misfortune I still regret, as the piece seemed to me one of his best.

Seamus Byrne, though frail, looked much younger than his years, and his death was surprising. He had talked of a new play, and two of his pieces have never yet reached print. The two which have, *Design for a Headstone* and *Little City,* seem to me among the most thoughtful and yet forceful pieces of their day; and the day of *Design for a Headstone* is far from over.

Jack White was the youngest of these playwrights to die, and his death was the most startling. He had quietly done four satisfying novels, a book about the Anglo-Irish, and two Abbey plays. His working life in radio and television was crowded, and one wishes that he had had time to write more, for what he has done is quite first-rate. Only one of his plays, *The Last Eleven,* has reached print. It won the Irish Life Drama award and was given an effective Abbey production in 1968 (a production, incidentally, which must have been the last time May Craig and Eileen Crowe appeared together). This quiet, telling, realistic study of a diminishing and decaying Church of Ireland congregation still remains one of the sturdiest works produced in the new Abbey Theatre.

III

This is primarily a book about the playwrights of the Irish theatre, but there were fine actors who died too — among them, Michael Conniffe, Harry Hutchinson, Harry Brogan, Eileen Crowe, May Craig, Angela Newman. This is no place to pay tribute to their fine talents, but the death in 1980 of the director Alan Simpson must be mentioned. If for no other reason than that he was often an unacknowledged, and brilliant, collaborator with his writers.

Simpson had many successes, and some of them outside of Ireland, but I think that it was not entirely realised in Ireland just how good he was. There is still probably a lingering notion that Carolyn Swift, that bright and able woman, was the brains behind the Pike. There is even the notion that poor, bumbling Alan managed good productions because the actors took pity on his hopeless fuddle and gave him utterly of their best. All of this seems to me nonsense.

For most of his twenty-five active years, Simpson had few rivals as the most dynamic director on the Irish stage. For perhaps about ten years of that time, Jim Fitzgerald certainly rivalled him. For much of that time, Hilton Edwards still worked with his meticulous craftsmanship. Barry Cassin did always conscientious work — and in the instance of Leonard's Joycean adaptation of *The Dead* memorable work. Tomás Mac Anna did a superb, and very Simpson-like job with *Borstal Boy*. Chloe Gibson did some solid work. Shelah Richards, who had done a lot of late directing for television, came up with a nearly consummate *Sharon's Grave* for the Irish Theatre Company. But nobody so consistently approached Simpson's dynamic, vigorous, free-wheeling direction.

He had his limitations, and they became ever more constricting towards the end of his life. He might have developed into a terrific *avant garde* director, for he had cut his teeth on Beckett before Beckett was fashionable. But he became ever more a purveyor of commercial dynamics, of rock musical spectaculars for Noel Pearson. And even earlier on, his production of Molloy's beautiful, melancholy *The Wood of the Whispering* for Joan Littlewood must have been a jaw-slackening disaster, for rarely could the strongest qualities of author and director have been so out of tune.

What he could do best was to manipulate crowds, to choreograph spectacles and − above all − to infuse a drive, a vigour, a buoyant vitality. The last show of his I saw combined all of those qualities. It was an Off-Off Broadway production at the Perry Street Theatre in Greenwich Village of *Androcles and the Lion*. My own feeling about directing Shaw is that tinkering with the script is pernicious folly, for Shaw knew better than any director what was going to work. Alan utterly Simpsonised *Androcles:* he cut at least a third and made it a mini-rock opera, with such gratuitously intruded jokes as an Emperor who, when he smiled suddenly became the spittin' image of Jimmy Carter. To a fervent Shavian, all of this show biz stuff was damn near sacrilegious. And yet the show was so bouncy, such fun and so totally theatrical that it was irresistible. The methods that worked so well and were so necessary for *The Scatterin'* or *Richard's Cork Leg* were neither appropriate nor needed for *Androcles*. But if Alan substituted his silver for Shaw's gold, his silver was newly minted, and there was an abundance of it. And for all of his career he gave it to us in profusion. We could have better spared, as Prince Hal said, a better man. Though where could we have found one?

But among theatre lovers, the deaths of Edwards and MacLiammóir must be those the most profoundly regretted. They were not, like Yeats, leaders of taste and founders of movements. Yet their energy, their dedication, their incredible conscientiousness in mounting a play, and their buoyant sense of the fun of the theatre did finally affect taste on both the stage and in the auditorium. What they could do well, they did better than anyone else in their time, and there was much that they could do well. Shelah Richards has written of "a sort of glamour and authenticity . . . and always a distinctive stamp to an Edwards–MacLiammóir production." For decades, those productions not only moved and entertained, but they also educated Dublin to new plays and new theatrical ways. They were the chief reason why, for fifty years, Dublin was theatrically something more than a provincial city, and their legacy is that they are still a chief reason why it is interesting today.

A CRITICAL APPENDIX,
BY W. J. LAWRENCE

The following notices and extracts are all taken from Lawrence's columns in the British publication, *The Stage,* and comprise a pretty typical selection of Lawrence's faults and qualities.

'BIRTHRIGHT' BY T. C. MURRAY (1910).

After much experimentation in divers genres, the Irish dramatist is beginning to find himself. It has dawned upon him that his is an agricultural, not a manufacturing country, and that the Irish national drama is the drama of peasant life. Within the last year or two Munster has made notable additions to the ranks of the new school of Irish playwrights by contributing recruits reared among the rural masses. Of these one of the most promising (judged by the observation and the technical skill he has already exhibited in *The Wheel of Fortune* and the latest new play), is Mr T. C. Murray, a County Cork school teacher. In *Birthright* he has written an up-to-date drama without expressing what up-to-date Irish plays, in G. Bernard Shaw's opinion, convey — 'the most furious detestation of Ireland'.

The theme about which he concerns himself, and in legal phrase 'states a case' with craftsmanship and cogency, is the ghastly irony of primogeniture. . . . With Mr. Murray's terse, well-knit play little fault can be found. It is a pity, however, that the action should gradually descend from the peaks of pure drama into the valleys of melodrama. Had the high plane of the first act been maintained, *Birthright* would have been a masterly work.

The chief acting honours of the evening fell to Mr. Sydney J. Morgan for his well-nigh flawless reading of the coarse, strong-willed old farmer. It is doubtful if an impersonation of equal forcefulness, faithfulness and power has been seen on the Abbey boards. . . . Several defects were to be marked in the general 'production' of the play, which Mr. S. L. Robinson, the stage manager and producer, should hasten to amend. As a Munsterman, he should be fully aware that the County Cork peasant follows the convention of the 'Sunday best', and lays by his workaday clothes on the day of rest. Again, the make-up of some of the characters was inconsistent with their relative ages. . . .

161

'THE MAGNANIMOUS LOVER' BY ST. JOHN ERVINE (1912)

On more than one occasion we have found it necessary to protest in these columns against the disposition of Abbey Theatre realists to indulge in offensive diction of a wholly gratuitous order, and we regret now the necessity which demands a severer condemnation. Hitherto our strictures have been levelled at the use and abuse of a certain sanguinary epithet common to the barrack-room and the street; but, ill in taste as is this adjective, it is not so gross to female ears as the old English vocable which Mr. St. John G. Ervine puts into the mouth of his principal female character in his new play. It is no excuse to say that Shakespeare makes Othello use the word in his great scene with Iago. No modern representative of the Moor since Edwin Forrest has ever dared to utter the phrase, and the usual custom has been to substitute the word 'wanton'.[1] Had the first-night audience exercised its prerogative and vigorously hissed this breach of good taste, we should not have dwelt upon the point; but, unfortunately, ever since Mr. Yeats called in the police to eject legitimate protestants against *The Playboy* the Abbey has failed to exercise its functions and permitted judgment to go by default. This is a parlous state of things in a country where there is no censorship. . . .

'THE MAGIC GLASSES' BY GEORGE FITZMAURICE (1913)

The industrious but somewhat too frank Press Agent of the Abbey Theatre, who stated in the preliminary notices of *The Magic Glasses* that it would probably mystify the Dublin audience, had sound reason for the faith within him. It did. Nobody could make head or tail of Mr. Fitzmaurice's jig-saw puzzle, which proved a wild and whirling waste of coruscating, multi-coloured words. Never, perhaps, in the wide annals of the stage was so little said at so great length. The story of the play, so far as it can be said to have a story, concerns itself with one Jaymony Shanahan, a thirty-year-old country lout, who has bought some magical musical glasses from a woman in a forest and who occupies himself all day in the loft above the family kitchen in playing upon these glasses and in gazing upon the magic pictures they show. His poor old father and mother call in a countryside quack, one Mr. Quille (in appearance a cross between an Abbey Theatre minor poet and a returned Irish-American), to cure him of his obsession. Quille goes through some monkey tricks, including a sham epileptic fit, and finally recommends the Shanahans to get Jaymony a wife. All that good acting could do was done for this amazing hotch-potch, but it was impossible to educe either humour or interest out of such mid-summer madness, and the whole fell as flat as a flounder. If *The Magic Glasses* had any chance of living one would strongly recommend Mr. Power to modify his extravagant make-up as Jaymony Shanahan, which was apparently based on the 'tramp cyclist' of the music halls.

'SHANWALLA' BY LADY GREGORY (1915)

Shanwalla is an amazing farrago to come from the practised pen of that gifted humorist, Lady Gregory, the chief director of the Abbey Theatre, and one of the leaders of that particular *coterie* of Irish 'literary' dramatists whose tenets comprise a profound contempt for Dion Boucicault and all his works. Although vaguely described in the bills as 'a play in three acts', the new Abbey production is rank melodrama of the crudest and most obsolete order. It is precisely the sort of thing that 'Monk' Lewis of *Castle Spectre* fame, would have written, with this distinction, that Lewis and his school knew how to move a horror skilfully. Boucicault at his worst never concocted anything half so preposterous, and at least his handling was never feeble. With his splendid sense of theatrical effect, one can surmise how eerie and enthralling a play he would have constructed on Lady Gregory's basic idea, which embodies the old superstition that spirits with something on their minds roam the world until relieved of their secret by the questioning of courageous mortals, and that the blind have psychic qualities denied to the majority of human beings. It is the ghost *motif* of *Hamlet* with up-to-date orchestration. Although approaching her theme with the reverential awe of the peasant, and embroidering upon it with such deadly seriousness that she suppresses throughout her relieving gifts of humour, Lady Gregory evinces so weak a sense of the theatre that the whole assumes the aspect of a travesty on ghost drama. Little wonder that in the last act, constituting in its cumulative absurdities one of the most amazing trial scenes ever witnessed on any stage, the audience laughed most irreverently at the spectre. . . .

'JUNO AND THE PAYCOCK' BY SEAN O'CASEY (1924)

. . . Years ago, when the Abbey was in its crudely experimental stage, Senator Yeats, in one of those delightful little impromptus with which he used to favour us between the acts, expressed the opinion that the prevailing dramatic moulds had become outworn, and that we in Ireland would have to break them and fashion moulds nearer to the heart's desire. If he is as strong a believer now as he was then in the necessity to go back to first principles, he, as chief director of the Abbey, should be proud of the vogue of Mr. O'Casey's plays. For Mr. O'Casey is at once inconoclast and neo-Elizabethan. One cannot place his plays in any recognised category. Nothing in Polonius's breathless, jaw-breaking list applies; and he flouts all the precepts of Aristotle. He lures us into the theatre under the pretext of affording us hearty laughter, which, sooth to say, he most profusely provokes, and he sends us away with tears in our eyes and with the impression of direst tragedy lying heavy on our hearts. None but a neo-Elizabethan could accomplish this, since the secret of juxtaposing and harmonising the comic with the tragic, and thereby throwing the elements of terror and pathos into greater comic relief, has been lost to the English-speaking stage for over a couple of centuries. Moreover, one-half of the fascination of Mr. O'Casey's work lies in its red-hot throbbing contemporaneity, and that too was a prime trait of Elizabethan drama. There are moments in his plays, such as the search of the Black-and-Tans in *The Shadow of a Gunman,* and the haling to death of the crippled informer, Johnny Boyle, in *Juno and the Paycock,* so vivid in the light of recent experience that they transcend all mere theatricality and thrill one to the marrow like matters of personal suffering. . . .

NOTES

YEATS CREATES A CRITIC

1 R. Hogan and M. J. O'Neill, eds., *Joseph Holloway's Theatre,* Vol. III (Dixon, California: Proscenium Press, 1970), pp. 46-47.
2 Unless otherwise noted, the remaining quotations in this chapter are gleaned from Lawrence's Personal Clippings Books which are contained in the National Library of Ireland.
3 *The Times,* 13 August 1940.
4 W. J. Lawrence, *Old Theatre Days and Ways.*
5 Mac [Isa MacNie], *The Celebrity Zoo* (Dublin: Browne & Nolan, 3rd edition, 1925), unpaginated.
6 R. Hogan & M. J. O'Neill, eds., *Joseph Holloway's Abbey Theatre* (Carbondale and Edwardsville: Southern Illinois University Press, 1967), p. 92.

THE INFLUENCE OF SYNGE

1 The Dublin Theatre Festival of 1981 has booked two Irish adaptations of Chekhov, one written by Brian Friel and produced by his Field Day Theatre company, and one written by Thomas Kilroy produced by the Irish Theatre Company and previously produced with some success in London. I should be surprised if either play is unsuccessful, but I am also surprised at the competent adaptors for attempting what could only be described as a rather perverse technical exercise. Addendum, 1982: Kilroy's was quite successful, Friel's not.
2 Austin Clarke, 'Introduction', *The Plays of George Fitzmaurice,* Vol. I (Dublin: The Dolmen Press, 1967), p. viii.
3 *Ibid.,* pp. 13-14.
4 Most of Fitzmaurice's not particularly notable stories are gathered in *The Crows of Mephistopheles* (Dublin: The Dolmen Press, 1970).
5 *The Plays of George Fitzmaurice,* Vol. II (Dublin: The Dolmen Press, 1969), p. 9.
6 Bryan MacMahon, 'Song of the Anvil', *Seven Irish Plays, 1946-1964,* ed. R. Hogan (Minneapolis: University of Minnesota Press, 1967), p. 223.
7 The speech is quoted from the unpublished manuscript of the play. Slightly altered, the speech may be found in the published novel version. See *The Honey Spike* (London: The Bodley Head, 1967), p. 245.
8 Michael Molloy, 'The Visiting House', *Seven Irish Plays,* p. 95.
9 Michael Molloy, 'The Paddy Pedlar', *Three Plays* (Newark, Delaware: Proscenium Press, 1975), p. 116.
10 John B. Keane, *Sive* (Dublin: Progress House, 1959), pp. 41-42,

THERE IS REALISM AND REALISM

1 Cornelius Weygandt, *Irish Plays and Playwrights* (Boston and New York: Houghton Mifflin, 1931.
2 Una Ellis-Fermor, *The Irish Dramatic Movement* (London: Methuen, 1971).
3 A similar awkwardness may be seen in the plays of George Moore, whether it be *The Strike at Arlingford* which he wrote on his own for the Independent Theatre in London, or his revision of Martyn's *Tale of a Town,* or his collaboration with Yeats in *Diarmuid and Grania.*

4   Gabriel Fallon, *Sean O'Casey, The Man I Knew* (London: Routledge and Kegan Paul), 1965.
5   Edward Martyn, *The Heather Field* (Chicago: De Paul University Press), p. 66.
6   J. Bernard MacCarthy, *Plays* (Dublin: M. H. Gill, 1936).
7   William Boyle, *The Building Fund* (Dublin: Maunsel, 1906), pp. 5-6. I have cited the second edition, as there are a number of cuts and changes between the first edition of 1905 and the second of 1906. Boyle further tinkered with the play, and even made a one-act version for the Fays to play in America.
8   William Boyle, *The Eloquent Dempsy* (Dublin: M. H. Gill, 1916), p. 22.
9   Padraic Colum, *Thomas Muskerry* (Dublin: Maunsel, 1910), pp. 3 & 5.
10 *Ibid.,* pp. 4-5.
11 *Ibid.,* p. 63.
12 *Ibid.,* p. 64
13 Andrew E. Malone, *The Irish Drama* (New York and London: Benjamin Blom, 1965).
14 Seumas O'Sullivan, *Essays and Recollections* (Dublin and Cork: The Talbot Press, 1944), pp. 118-119.
15 Seumas O'Kelly, *The Shuiler's Child* (Dublin: Maunsel, 1909), pp. 51-52.
16 Seumas O'Kelly, *Meadowsweet* (Naas: The Leinster Leader, n.d.), pp. 10-11.
17 St. John Ervine, *Four Irish Plays* (Dublin: Maunsel, 1914).
18 *Ibid.*
19 St. John Ervine, *John Ferguson* (New York: Macmillan, 1923), pp. 85-86.

O'CASEY, THE STYLE AND THE ARTIST

1   Moody Prior, *The Language of Tragedy* (Gloucester, Mass.: Peter Smith, 1964), p. 310.
2   John Gassner, 'Genius Without Fetters', *Selected Plays of Sean O'Casey* (New York: George Braziller, 1954), p. xx.
3   There was an interesting exchange of letters on this point between Murray and O'Casey in *The Irish Press* in 1941. The letters are reproduced in *Joseph Holloway's Irish Theatre,* Vol. III (Dixon, California: Proscenium Press, 1970), pp. 54-56.
4   There is also the extended parody in Act One of *The Drums of Father Ned* of a patriotic melodrama à la Boucicault − or, more properly, à la J. W. Whitbread, Ira Allen or P. J. Bourke.
5   O'Casey in various places creates quite a pantheon of such saints. There is also in this play a mention of St. Crankarious; there is the statue of St. Temolo in *The Bishop's Bonfire;* there is St. Sinfoilio in *Behind the Green Curtains.* An allied device is the symbolic portmanteau name. In this play, One-eyed Larry mentions the terrible spirits Kissalass, Velvethighs, Reedabuck, Dancesolong, and Sameagain. In *Behind the Green Curtains,* Beoman refers to the 'blessed saints' of religious reaction − Stepaside, Touchnrun, Dubudont, and Goslow. There are many other instances, especially in the autobiographies.
6   A slightly phonetic spelling of the Dublin pronunciation of 'Trent'.
7   The first stanza of Fraser's poem reads:

> Come pledge again thy heart and hand −
> One grasp that ne'er shall sever:
> Our watchword be 'Our native land' −
> Our motto, 'Love for ever.'
> And let the Orange lily be
> *Thy* badge, my patriot brother −
> The everlasting Green for me;
> And we for one another.

The poem is most easily obtainable in the collection *The Spirit of the Nation,* which is published by James Duffy of Dublin, and which has gone through about sixty editions.

8 The entire poem may be found in *The First Book of Irish Ballads,* edited by Daniel O'Keefe (Cork: The Mercier Press, 1955), p. 41.

9 Reprinted in *The Spirit of the Nation.*

10 Mrs. De Burgh Daly, ed., *Prose, Poems and Parodies of Percy French* (Dublin: The Talbot Press, 1962), pp. 6-7.

11 *The National & Historical Ballads of Ireland* (Glasgow: Cameron, Ferguson & Co., n.d.), pp. 143-44.

O'CASEY, THE STYLE AND THE MAN

1 Sean O'Casey, *The Flying Wasp* (London: Macmillan, 1937), p. 80.

2 *Ibid.,* p. 152.

3 Sean O'Casey, *I Knock at the Door,* Part One of *Mirror in My House,* Vol. I (New York: Macmillan, 1956), pp. 3-4.

4 Sean O'Casey, *Blasts and Benedictions,* edited by Ronald Ayling (London: Macmillan; New York: St. Martin's Press, 1967), p. 76.

THE INFLUENCE OF O'CASEY

1 *Anti-Christ* has not been published, but the manuscript may be read at the National Library of Ireland.

2 Robert Hogan, *The Experiments of Sean O'Casey* (New York: St. Martin's Press, 1960), p. 144.

DENIS JOHNSTON'S HORSE LAUGH

1 Denis Johnston, 'Humor − Hibernian Style', *The New York Times* (5 February 1961), Sect. 2, p. 3.

2 One is reminded of the great F. J. McCormick, who played Johnston's Dobelle, coming before the rioting audience of O'Casey's *The Plough and the Stars* to hope the audience would not identify the actors with their roles.

3 Denis Johnston, 'Let There be Light', *The Old Lady Says 'No!' and Other Plays* (Boston: Little Brown, 1960).

4 R Hogan and M. J. O'Neill, eds., *Joseph Holloway's Irish Theatre,* Vol. I (Dixon, California: Proscenium Press, 1968), p. 75.

5 On the same day, the Guild gave in Boston the world première of Shaw's *Too True to be Good,* and this review appeared above Johnston's.

6 J. B., 'The Guild Goes Irish', *The New York Times* (1 March 1932), p. 19.

7 J. Brooks Atkinson, 'With Its Irish Up', *The New York Times* (13 March 1932), Sect. 8, p. 1.

8 'Westminster Theatre', *The Times* (25 September 1934), p. 12.

9 'Haymarket Theatre', *The Times* (24 November 1934), p. 10.

10 Howard Taubman, 'The Theatre: Irish Irony', *The New York Times* (7 February 1961), p. 40.

11 Denis Johnston, *The Old Lady Says 'No!' and Other Plays.*

TRYING TO LIKE BECKETT

1 John Fletcher, *Samuel Beckett's Art* (London: Chatto & Windus, 1967), p. 146.

2 Jean Anouilh, quoted in *Samuel Beckett, the Critical Heritage,* edited by L. Grover and R. Federman (London: Routledge and Kegan Paul, 1979), p. 92.

3 Harold Hobson, 'The First Night of "Waiting for Godot" ', *Beckett at 60* (London: Calder and Boyars, 1967), p. 25

4   Harold Pinter, 'Beckett', *Beckett at 60,* p. 86.
5   Ruby Cohn, *Back to Beckett* (Princeton: Princeton University Press, 1973), pp. 7 passim.
6   Martin Esslin, ed., *Samuel Beckett, A Collection of Critical Essays* (Englewood Cliffs, N. J.: Prentice-Hall, 1965), p.14.

SINCE O'CASEY

1   I had, in an earlier version of this piece, written 'changed, changed irritably', and a young critic took me up on that, charging, I suppose, American-Irish nostalgia. As I have always thought that American-Irishness was disgusting and made stage-Irishness look realistic, I have revised my phrase, as I am here interested in recording a fact rather than indulging a sentiment.
2   One extraordinary exception would be Patricia Finney's retelling of the Cuchulain story in her novels *A Shadow of Gulls* (1977) and *The Crow Goddess* (1978).
3   In 1982, the Arts Council announced that it would no longer fund the I.T.C., and that after 1982 it would no longer fund the Theatre Festival. At this writing, both decisions are being contested.
4   *The Times,* 14 May 1981.
5   The problem of communication is central to innumerable plays, whether it be the mistaken identities of farce or the misunderstood identities of Oedipus or Hamlet. Even commercial Broadways plays, such as *Butterflies Are Free* which dealt with blindness, or *Children of a Lesser God* which dealt with deafness, have taken up the theme of how love can create a language.
6   Friel has certainly demonstrated that he can develop a plot. See, for instance, *The Enemy Within* which was a very early play. Sometimes, however, he gives plot short shrift and usually to the detriment of the play. See *The Loves of Cass Maguire* and see particularly *Volunteers.*
7   Leonard re-used the material of *Da* for his fictionalised memoir, *Home Before Night,* and used it with even greater success. Indeed, any reservations one might have about the play are fairly well swept away by the memoir, which has all the appearance of a minor classic.
8   Thomas Murphy, *A Crucial Week in the Life of a Grocer's Assistant* (Dublin: Gallery Books, 1978), p. 74
9   Thomas Murphy, *Famine* (Dublin: Gallery Books, 1977), p. 86.
10 Thomas Kilroy, *Talbot's Box* (Dublin: Gallery Books; Newark, Delaware: Proscenium Press, 1979), pp. 62.
11 Eugene McCabe, *Roma* (Dublin: Turoe Press, 1979), p. 44.
12 Liam Mac Uistin, *Post Mortem* (Newark, Delaware: Proscenium Press, 1977), pp. 8-9.
13 *Dictionary of Irish Literature* (Westport, Conn.: Greenwood Press, 1979), p. 256.
14 *Ibid,* p. 428.
15 Heno Magee, *Hatchet* (Dublin: Gallery Press; Newark, Delaware: Proscenium Press, 1978), pp. 15-16.
16 Maeve Binchy, *Deeply Regretted By* (Dublin: Turoe Press, 1979), pp. 57-58.

A FACTUAL APPENDIX

1   Indeed, McCann's performance in the last five minutes of Friel's *Faith Healer* is probably the most rivetting piece of acting I have ever seen on the Abbey stage. The actor created an astonishing intensity and yet seemed to be doing practically nothing. He arrested a gesture with his right hand, he stood nearly stockstill, his voice was not pushed — and yet somehow the effect was hypnotic. For the most part, McCann's approach to a role seems like Cyril Cusack's work in the last twenty years or so. The parts are played with a consummate subtlety, but not hugely differentiated. Kavanagh's approach is quite different,

and each new part will show, in its gait and its gestures and its voice, a distinctly new creation. McCann's roles are all brothers, but Kavanagh's Master of Ceremonies in *Cabaret,* his Hatchet in Heno Magee's play, and his Casimir in Friel's *Aristocrats* are each distinctly individual. Like McCann, he can invest a weak part, such as the drunken son in William Trevor's *Scenes from an Album* with strength. While McCann seems a follower of Cusack, Kavanagh seems a character actor in the eclectic style of F. J. McCormick; and both seem eminently capable of extending the tradition of great Irish character acting through this generation.

INDEX

Index   173

Hauptmann, Gerhart, *The Weavers,* 44
Hayes, David, 146, 147; *Sorry! No Hard Feelings?,* 147
Healy, Gerard, *Thy Dear Father,* 58
Hemingway, Ernest, *Across the River and Into the Trees,* 80; *For Whom the Bell Tolls,* 80; *The Green Hills of Africa,* 80; *The Sun Also Rises,* 80
Henderson, W. A., 21, 89
Hogan J. J., 17–18
Hogan, Robert, 28; *After the Irish Renaissance,* 136
Holloway, Joseph, 11–12, 20, 21, 24, 99, 119
Howard, Sidney, *They Knew What They Wanted,* 140
Hutchinson, Ron, *Says I, Says He,* 143
Hyde, Douglas, 11, 29, 31

Ibsen, Henrik, 44, 94; *A Doll's House,* 28, 57; *An Enemy of the People,* 43 *The Lady from the Sea,* 43
Irish Academy of Letters, 136, 150
Irish Arts Center (New York), 147
Irish Literary Society, 73
Irish Times, 13, 140, 152
Irish Theatre Company, 125, 139, 142, 156, 159, 168

Johnson, Samuel, 78, 79
Johnston, Denis, 96–112, 154; (with Ernst Toller) *Blind Man's Buff,* 97; *A Bride for the Unicorn,* 97, 98; *The Dreaming Dust,* 97, 98, 103; *The Golden Cuckoo,* 97, 98; *The Moon in the Yellow River,* 96–112 *passim; The Old Lady Says 'No!',* 27, 97, 98, 104, 110; *The Scythe and the Sunset,* 97; *'Strange Occurrence on Ireland's Eye',* 97
Jonson, Ben, 89, *Volpone,* 105
Journal of Irish Literature, 51, 144
Joyce, James, 51, 71, 80, 88, 115, 159; *Finnegans Wake,* 90, 116; *Ulysses,* 90, 126
Judge, Michael, 146–47; *Harbour Hotel,* 146; *Saturday Night Women,* 45, 146

Kaufman, George S., *Merrily We Roll Along,* 133
Kavanagh, Patrick, 11; *Tarry Flynn* (adapted by P. J. O'Connor), 126
Keane, John B., 34, 39, 40, 121, 144–46; *Big Maggie,* 39, 144, 145; *The Buds of Ballybunnion,* 146; *The Change in Mame Fadden,* 144, 145; *The Chastitute,* 144, 145–46; *The Crazy Wall,* 146; *The Field,* 39, 55, 144; *The Good Thing,* 39, 144, 145, 146; *The Highest House on the Mountain,* 39; *Hut 42,* 39; *Letters of an Irish Minister of State,* 145; *Letters of an Irish T.D.,* 145; *Many Young Men of Twenty,* 57; *Sharon's Grave,* 39–40, 144; *Sive,* 39, 40, 144; *Values,* 146; *The Year of the Hiker,* 130, 144
Keily, Benedict, *Proxopera* (dramatised by Peter Luke), 143
Kelly, Seamus, 140
Kickham, Charles J., 'Rory of the Hill', 75–76
Kilroy, Tom, 121, 136, 138–40, 148, 156; *The Big Chapel,* 139; *The Life and Resurrection of Mr. Roche,* 139; *The O'Neill,* 139, *Talbot's Box,* 140; *Tea and Sex and Shakespeare,* 122, 139
Knoblock, Ernest, *Kismet,* 50

Labiche, Eugène, *Célimare,* 132
Lamb, Randal M., 88
Lantern Theatre (Dublin), 80, 157
Lawrence, D. H., *The Widowing of Mrs. Holroyd,* 30
Lawrence, W. J., 11–12, 13–24, 161–64; *Annals of the Old Belfast Stage,* 15; *Barry Sullivan,* 15; *The Elizabethan Playhouse,* 13, 14, 16; *The Life of G. V. Brooke,* 15; *Old Theatre Days and Ways,* 17,18; *The Physical Conditions of the Elizabethan Playhouse,* 13, 16; *Pre-Restoration Stage Studies,* 13, 17; *Shakespeare's Lost Hamlet,* 17; *Shakespeare's Workshop,* 17; *Speeding up Shakespeare,* 17; *Those Nut-Cracking Elizabethans,* 17
Leonard, Hugh, 41, 121, 132–36, 144, 145, 148, 159, 165; *The Au Pair Man,* 133; *Da,* 132, 134–35, 168; *Home Before Night,* 168; *A Leap in the Dark,* 134; *A Life,* 130, 132, 134, 135; *Madigan's Lock,* 134; *Mick and Mick,* 134; *The Patrick Pearse Motel,* 133; *The Poker Session,* 134; *Summer,* 132, 134; *Time Was,* 134; *When the Saints Go Cycling In* (after Flann O'Brien), 127, 133